ECOLE
DE
CAVALERIE

C. Parrocel inv.   B. Audran Sculp.

Copyright © 1992 by Xenophon Press
Copyright © 2015 by Xenophon Press LLC

Illustrated by Charles Parocel

Translation from French Copyright © 1978 and 1979 by EDA Corp.

Additional Chapters Translated by Richard F. Williams

Appendix from Part I: Chapter VI translated by Danielle Goulding

Edited by Richard F. Williams and Frances A. Williams, M.D.

All rights reserved. No part of this work may be reproduced or transmitted in any form or by any means, electronic or mechanical, including photocopying and recording, or by any information storage or retrieval system, except as may be expressly permitted by the 1976 Copyright Act or in writing from the publisher. Requests for permission should be addressed in writing to Xenophon Press LLC, 7518 Bayside Road, Franktown Virginia USA 94044-2106

www.XenophonPress.com   xenophonpress@gmail.com.

Published by Xenophon Press LLC

7518 Bayside Road, Franktown, Virginia 23354-2106, U.S.A.

Previous ISBN-13: 9780933316010
Print ISBN-13: 9780933316690
ebook ISBN-13: 9780933316706

Cover drawing: Detail of "Scène de bataille" by Jacques Gamelin, last quarter of the 18th century, © Musée du Vieux-Toulouse, France.

ÉCOLE DE CAVALERIE

The Expanded, Complete Edition
of
PART II :
The Method of Training Horses,
According to the Different Ways
in Which They Will be Used.
with
An Appendix from Part I:
Chapter VI On the Bridle

by FRANÇOIS ROBICHON
de la GUÉRINIÈRE

© Xenophon Press 1992
© Xenophon Press 2015

XENOPHON PRESS LIBRARY

Xenophon Press is dedicated to the preservation of classical equestrian literature. We bring both new and old works to English-speaking riders. Available at www.XenophonPress.com

30 Years with Master Nuno Oliveira, Henriquet 2011
A New Method to Dress Horses, Cavendish 2015
A Rider's Survival from Tyranny, de Kunffy 2012
Another Horsemanship, Racinet 1994
Art of the Lusitano, Yglesias de Oliveira 2012
Austrian Art of Riding, Poscharnigg 2015
Breaking and Riding, Fillis 2015
Baucher and His School, Decarpentry 2011
Dressage in the French Tradition, Diogo de Bragança 2011
Dressage Principles Illuminated, Expanded Edition, de Kunffy 2015
École de Cavalerie Part II, Robichon de la Guérinière 1992, 2015
Equine Osteopathy: What the Horses Have Told Me, Ginaux 2014
François Baucher: The Man and His Method, Baucher/Nelson 2013
Great Horsewomen of the 19th Century in the Circus, Nelson 2015
Gymnastic Exercises for Horses Volume II, Russell 2013
H. Dv. 12 Cavalry Manual of Horsemanship, Reinhold 2014
Handbook of Jumping Essentials, Lemaire de Ruffieu 1997
Handbook of Riding Essentials, Lemaire de Ruffieu 2015
Healing Hands, Giniaux, DVM 1998
Horse Training: Outdoors and High School, Beudant 2014
Legacy of Master Nuno Oliveira, Millham 2013
Manege Moderne, D'Eisenberg 2015
Methodical Dressage of the Riding Horse, Faverot de Kerbrech 2010
Racinet Explains Baucher, Racinet 1997
Science and Art of Riding in Lightness, Stodulka 2015
The Art and Science of Riding in Lightness, Stodulka 2014
The Art of Traditional Dressage, Volume I DVD, de Kunffy 2013
The Ethics and Passions of Dressage Expanded Ed., de Kunffy 2013
The Gymnasium of the Horse, Steinbrecht 2011
The Italian Tradition of Equestrian Art, Tomassini 2014
The Maneige Royal, de Pluvinel 2010
The Portuguese School of Equestrian Art, de Oliveira/da Costa 2012
The Spanish Riding School & Piaffe and Passage, Decarpentry 2013
To Amaze the People with Pleasure and Delight, Walker 2015
Total Horsemanship, Racinet 1999
Wisdom of Master Nuno Oliveira, de Coux 2012

TABLE OF CONTENTS

About the Author and His Book   v

PREFACE   viii

The Name and Position of the Exterior Parts of the Horse   xii

CHAPTER I	Why There Are So Few Horsemen & the Qualities Necessary to Become One	1
CHAPTER II	The Different Temperaments in Horses; the Cause of Their Indocility & the Vices That Result	4
CHAPTER III	The Instruments Used in Training Horses	7
CHAPTER IV	The Terms of the Art	12
CHAPTER V	The Different Movements of the Legs of the Horse and the Difference in Their Gaits	16

   FIRST ARTICLE: *The Natural Gaits*   18
      The Walk   18
      The Trot   18
      The Canter   18
      False and Disunited Canters   23
      The False Canter (Counter Canter)   23
      The Disunited Canter   24
   ARTICLE II: *The Defective Gaits*   24
      The Amble   24
      The Single-foot or Traguenard   26
      The Aubin   26
   ARTICLE III: *The Artificial Gaits*   27
   The Low Airs or Figures on the Ground   27
      The Passage   27
      The Piaffe   29
      The Galopade   29
      The Change of Hand   29
      The Volte   31
      The Passade   31
      The Pirouette   31
      The Terre à Terre   31
   The High Airs or Airs Above the Ground   33
      The Pesade   33
      The Mézair   33
      The Courbette   33
      The Croupade   33
      The Ballotade   37

	The Capriole	*37*
	The Pas & le Saut (The step and jump)	*37*
CHAPTER VI	*On Acquiring a Good Seat & Things to Observe Before Mounting*	*38*
CHAPTER VII	*The Bridle Hand and Its Effects*	*42*
CHAPTER VIII	*The Aids and Punishments Required to Train Horses*	*47*
	The Aids	*47*
	The Punishments	*49*
	The Long Whip	*49*
	The Switch	*50*
	The Spurs	*50*
CHAPTER IX	*The Necessity of the Trot in Suppling Young Horses & The Benefits of The Walk*	*52*
	The Walk	*56*
CHAPTER X	*On The Halt, The Half-Halt, & The Rein Back*	*58*
	On the Halt	*58*
	On the Half-Halt	*60*
	On the Rein Back	*61*
CHAPTER XI	*On The Shoulder-In*	*63*
CHAPTER XII	*On The Croup to The Wall (Haunches-Out)*	*71*
CHAPTER XIII	*On The Usefulness of The Pillars*	*77*
CHAPTER XIV	*On The Passage*	*82*
CHAPTER XV	*Changes of Hand and the Way to* Doubler	*87*
CHAPTER XVI	*On The Canter*	*91*
CHAPTER XVII	*On Voltes, Half-Voltes, Passades, Pirouettes, & the* Terre-A-Terre	*96*
FIRST ARTICLE: *On Voltes*		*96*
ARTICLE II: *On the Half-Voltes*		*101*
ARTICLE III: *On Passades*		*103*
ARTICLE IV: *On The Pirouette*		*104*
ARTICLE V: *On the* Terre-a-Terre		*105*
CHAPTER XVIII	*On the Airs above the Ground*	*108*
FIRST ARTICLE: *On the Pesade*		*109*
ARTICLE II: *On the Mézair*		*111*
ARTICLE III: *On the Courbette*		*113*
ARTICLE IV: *On the Croupade and the Ballotade*		*116*
ARTICLE V: *On the Caprioles*		*118*
The "Pas-et-le-Saut" & The "Galop-Gaillard" (Step and Jump & Strong, Vigorous Canter)		*119*
CHAPTER XIX	*On War Horses*	*122*

CHAPTER XX	*On the Hunting Horse*	*127*
CHAPTER XXI	*On Carriage Horses*	*133*
CHAPTER XXII	*On tournaments, jousts, carousels, and contests*	*135*
FIRST ARTICLE:	*On Tournaments*	*136*
SECOND ARTICLE:	*On Jousts*	*137*
THIRD ARTICLE:	*On Carousels*	*137*
ARTICLE IV:	*On the contests*	*140*
ARTICLE V:	*On the head contest*	*141*
ARTICLE VI:	*The Ring Contest*	*145*
ARTICLE VII:	*The Foule Contest*	*147*

APPENDIX *from* PART I: CHAPTER XXII *On the Bridle*		*148*
FIRST ARTICLE:	*Of the Bit*	*149*
SECOND ARTICLE:	*Of the Branche (Shank)*	*151*
THIRD ARTICLE:	*Of the Gourmette (Curb Chain)*	*153*
ARTICLE IV:	*The Manner to Direct the Bridle According to the Difference in Mouths*	*153*
	Mouths Too Sensitive	*154*
	Weak Mouths	*155*
	Strong Mouths	*156*
	Heavy Mouths	*156*
	Mouths with Too Little or Tool Long Slits	*157*
	Horses Which Arm [Brace]	*157*

François Robichon de la Guerinière

ABOUT THE AUTHOR AND HIS BOOK

François Robichon de la Guérinière (1688-1751) was born in Essay, a small town near Alençon, where his father was a lawyer; he was also an officer at the court of the Duchess of Orleans. La Guérinière was a pupil of Antoine de Vendeuil, who was *"Écuyer ordinaire de la grande ecurie"* in Versailles between 1680 and 1717. In 1715, de la Guérinière received the title as *"Écuyer du Roi,"* which entitled him to give lessons. In 1730, Prince Charles of Lorraine, *"Grand Écuyer de France"* (Master of the Horse) named him director of the Royal Stables at the Tuileries, which had been founded by Antoine de Pluvinel, Louis XIII's teacher. De Pluvinel is best know for his work: *The Maneige Royal*, 1626 [Xenophon Press 2010].

La Guérinière's book, *École de Cavalerie*, was first published in 1731 and again under different titles between 1733 and 1802. It consists of three parts: Knowledge of the Horse In and Out of the Stable; Training; and Treatment of Illness.

This expanded volume contains all Chapters I - XXII of the Second Part of *École de Cavalerie*, entitled *De La Manière de Dresser Les Chevaux, Suivant Les Diferens Usages Auxquels On Les Destine.* (The Method of Training Horses According to the Different Ways in Which They Will Be Used). Chapters XIX through XXII are new to this edition and contain valuable information pertinent to today's riders and trainers. In discussing subjects as the training of the war horse, the hunt horse, the coach horse and other matters such as tournaments, jousting, carousels, etc., the author reveals important training advice that will be invaluable to riders of many disciplines. The illustrations used are reproduced from the 1733 edition. Further expanding this edition is an Appendix including a new translation of Chapter VI from Part I: *On the bridle*. Part II, the training portion of the three volume book heavily references the bridle and the use of the rider's hands. As editor, I felt it was important to include these detailed descriptions and recommendations of the time as most are completely applicable to today's rides especially with the interest in historic bits, bridles and equipment.

The late Dr. Henri L. M. van Schaik, who most kindly reviewed this translation and made invaluable suggestions to help translate some rather archaic French terms into English to be understood by today's readers, in his book *Misconceptions and Simple Truths in Dressage*, [Xenophon Press 2016] mentions, in the biographical note on La Guérinière in the Index Nominum, that

"Notwithstanding the fact that his reputation as an extraordinary teacher had become international and that he received pupils from all over Europe, he was most of the time in financial trouble. Evidently, La Guérinière was not a good businessman. In 1731, he published his book, *École de Cavalerie*. In contrast to most of his predecessors, la

Guérinière was evidently a very methodical man. While Salomon de La Broue, Antoine de Pluvinel and the Duke of Newcastle ramble along and are very repetitious, La Guérinière has a strict scheme and stays with it. What contributed mostly to La Guérinière's fame was the fact that he invented the shoulder-in."

École de Cavalerie is one of the best works on equitation ever to appear in France. In fact, it would not be an exaggeration to say that after a long struggle beginning in the renaissance academies of Italy, equitation in France suddenly flowed forth from La Guérinière. To quote the late Head of the Spanish Court Riding School in Vienna, Colonel Alois Podhajsky,

"It was the great riding master La Guérinière who produced the most revolutionary book on riding of all time. Unlike [those by] his predecessors, his book is clear and easy to understand. He based it on simplicity and facts, in order to be completely understood by his readers." His principles are still "applied unaltered at the Spanish Court Riding School and may be seen there in daily use."

It is for these reasons that La Guérinière is considered the Father of French Equitation and the Father of Modern Dressage; and it is impossible to read a book about dressage without finding his name mentioned, credit given to him, and an occasional quote from his work. Thus, the serious horse-person who takes the time to read La Guérinière's work cannot help but enrich his/her own knowledge by discovering the depth and quality of information that forms the base of much of our equestrian theory.

By keeping this translation as literal as possible, we hope the reader will note that the vast majority of aspects of La Guérinière's teachings still hold true in modern practice. We are pleased to offer this newly expanded edition with the inclusion of all of the chapters of Part II, Appendix, large reproductions of the engravings, enhanced footnotes and definitions for today's readers.

This publication represents part of Xenophon Press' large mission of protecting and preserving the gems of horsemanship non-fiction. Xenophon Press is committed to bringing even more works from the past to light in the English language. Look for more new, old works to be translated and published in the future.

Richard F. Williams
Publisher
Xenophon Press LLC

ECOLE
DE CAVALERIE;
CONTENANT
LA CONNOISSANCE,
L'INSTRUCTION,
ET LA CONSERVATION
DU CHEVAL

Par M. DE LA GUERINIERE, *Ecuyer du Roi,*

TOME PREMIE

M. DCC. XXXVI

AVEC APPROBATION ET PRIVILEGE DU ROI

PREFACE

I will not do here, as many authors have done in the past, praise an exercise [the pursuit of horsemanship], which at all times has been called the most noble and the most useful. I will simply state that my intention in composing this work was to assemble in methodical order the principles that could facilitate the amateurs of horsemanship[1], the knowledge of all that is related to it.

As we know, this Art contains three essential topics, which are: the knowledge of the horse, the way to train him[2], and his conservation. It is also these three topics that are the subject of this work, which I have divided into three sections.

In the first one, I give the name and locations of the exterior parts of the horse, with its beauty and faults. I address the age, the difference in type of coat, horses from different countries, the bridle, the shoeing and the saddle.

The second section contains the principles for training horses, either for the arena, for war, for hunting or driving a coach. In fewer words: depending on the different uses that we expect from them. I added to this section a treatise on tournaments, jousts, carousels, and the head and ring races.

The third section [not included in this edition] contains osteology of the horse, the definitions of his sicknesses, the drugs to treat them, with a treatise of the surgeries practiced on that animal. I must warn the reader that I have no contribution to it. One must be knowledgeable in the matters concerning anatomy and medicine to take on treating this topic; otherwise one would fall into the common error of authors who have described equine illnesses. This error is to give confusing or false definitions and remedies which by their multiplicity will often destroy each other. It is in order to avoid these very dangerous inconveniences that I have sought a doctor from the Faculty [of medicine] (for example Edouard, first doctor of Henry IV whom the King had ordered to pursue this matter) has kindly agreed to use his care and talents to keep perfecting an enterprise, which was interrupted almost as soon as it started due to the unexpected death of this Prince.

---

1   *Cavalerie*
2   The word "horse" in French, *le cheval*, is masculine; so for the purpose of an accurate translation we have used the pronouns: "he" or "his" to refer to the horse as required.—*Editor's note.*

I naturally admit that it is not from my own personal source that I brought these principles that are used in this treatise. I have not only drawn whatever was good from the best authors on this subject, but I also consulted with people who, through their extensive experience have acquired the reputation of being true experts. It's with these credentials that I dare place before these rules and principles; hence the theory is most accurate, since it is based on the authority and the practice of Masters in this Art. So I limit myself in my work, to develop as much as possible, the truth, the simplicity, and the usefulness of this Art, to spare the amateurs of horsemanship the boring dissertations and the often repeated topics that we have heard from most authors before me. Far from embracing everything, they covered only one part. Not only did I apply myself to give clear, clean and precise definitions; but making them more understandable, I added to this work, pictures that will bring up and iron out all difficulties. Pictures become infinitely more sensible in these matters than everything we describe in verbal terms. It's according to these originals and under the direction of Monsieur Parrocel, regular painter of the King, and from the Royal Academy, whose reputation in this area is widely-known, that we have engraved the different areas of the arena that you will find in the second section. I also included floor plans, in order to see the proportion of the area we must observe to soften and work the horse indifferent ways.

Finally, I used everything to rejuvenate this ancient pursuit that reigned during the days of the Cavalerie. It is with this view that I sought to unveil the mysteries that seem to be reserved for a very small number of people; as if the truth should not spread universally and that the subtlety of this Art belongs absolutely only to those who are said to be "children of the ball."[3]

To our shame, we must admit that the love of the true beauty of this exercise has truly diminished. Today, we actually content ourselves with sloppier equitation. Too often riders neglect to seek the beautiful appearance that, in earlier times, we aspired to which brilliantly adorned our arenas, military revues, pageants and parades.

One should not blame this negligence, neither the lack of merit, nor the little attention of the ones at the head of the establishment assigned to instruct the nobles; the justice that the public gives them is proof of their ability. May I be allowed, as a gesture of honest recognition, to add my homage to one of the people whom, with knowledge of the cause, have praised Monsieur de Vendeuil, my illustrious Master. This particular homage I owe to him, to whom I owe everything, does

---

3   les Enfants de la balle, [a privileged few]

not affect my esteem for the other people in the same career. Monsieur de Vendeuil is one of the precious few remaining of the illustrious men before him whom the memory of will always be dear to whoever follows in their footsteps. Monsieur de Vendeuil knew how to combine the grace and the precision of Monsieur du Plessis, to the brilliant execution of Monsieur de la Vallée. Monsieur de Vendeuil is a person whose name and reputation will endure throughout the history of the pursuit of horsemanship.

François Robichon de la Guérinière

ECOLE DE CAVALERIE.

SECONDE PARTIE.
De la manière de dresser les Chevaux,
suivant les différents usages
auxquels on les destine.

SCHOOL OF HORSEMANSHIP

PART II.
The method of training Horses,
according to the different ways
in which they will be used.

The Forehand

The Forehead.................1
Temples........................2
Eye Sockets..................3
Lower Jaw....................4
Lips...............................5
Nostrils.........................6
Muzzle..........................7
Chin..............................8
Chin groove.................9
Neck............................10
Mane...........................11
Forelock......................12
Throat..........................13
Withers........................14
Shoulders....................15
Chest............................16
Elbow...........................17
Forearm.......................18
Vein of the Forearm....19
Chestnut......................20
Knee.............................21
Cannon........................22
Tendon........................23
Fetlock Joint................24
Fetlock.........................25
Pastern........................26
Coronet Band..............27
Hoof.............................28
Quarters......................29
Toe...............................30
Heel.............................31

The Body

Loins or Back..............32
Kidneys........................33
Sides............................34
Belly.............................35
Flanks..........................36

The Hindquarters

Croup...........................37
Dock of Tail................38
Buttocks......................39
Haunches....................40
Stifle............................41
Gaskin.........................42
Hock............................43
Chestnut......................44
Point of the Hock.......45

The Name and Position of the Exterior Parts of the Horse

CHAPTER I

Why *There Are So Few Horsemen* & the Qualities Necessary to Become One

All arts and sciences have principles and rules governing the methods resulting in those discoveries that lead to their perfection. The Cavalry is the only art for which it seems there is only need of practice; however, the practice, stripped of sound principles, is nothing more than routine that only results in a forced and uncertain performance and a false brilliance that fascinates the demi-connoisseurs, who are often amazed by the horse's kindness, rather than by the rider's skill. This is the reason for the small number of well-trained horses and the lack of ability presently seen in the majority of those people who call themselves horsemen.

This lack of principles indicates that the students are not at all able to distinguish between faults and perfection. Their only resource is imitation, and, unfortunately, it is definitely much easier to turn to false practice than to achieve what is correct.

Some who want to imitate those who seek to bring forth all the brilliance present in a horse, fall into the habit of continuously moving their hands and legs, which detracts from the rider's grace, causes the horse to assume a false posture, creates a false contact with the mouth, and makes the horse unsteady on his legs.

Others make a point of seeking the precision and accuracy they observe in those who have the awareness necessary to choose the horse, which naturally has an excellent mouth, solid haunches, and supple and controlled strength, qualities found in very few horses. Thus it is that those who imitate this accuracy, which is so highly sought after, break a bold horse's courage and destroy his natural kindness.

Still others, swept along by the supposed good taste of the public, whose decisions are not always from the oracles and against whom timid truth dares not revolt, find that after a lengthy and diligent pursuit, their only attainment is the flattering and chimeric satisfaction of thinking themselves more expert than the others.

Our great masters of the art (Monsieur du Plessis and the de la Vallée brothers), who had much to say during the successful days of the Cavalry and whose loss is regretted by many today, in no way entrusted us with rules that would direct us to what they had acquired through an unending diligence supported by good intentions, maintained by emulation of the nobility, and motivated by the view of a reward inseparable from true merit. Given the fact that it is difficult to attain the degree of perfection that they cultivated within the Cavalry, the decadence of such a noble discipline must be attributed more to the scarcity of models left to us than to carelessness on our part.

Deprived of these advantages, we can only look for the truth in the principles left to us by those who have written about their insights and the results of their work. From the large number of authors, there are only two whose works are agreed to be valuable by all the connoisseurs. They are Salomon de la Broue [c.1530-c.1610] and the Duke of Newcastle [1592-1676.]

De la Broue lived during the reign of Henry IV [1553-1610.] He composed a book that contains the principles of Giovanni Battista Pignatelli (c.1525-c.1600), his master, who was the head of an academy in Naples. This school was held in such high esteem that it was regarded as the best in the world. All of the French and German nobility who wanted to improve their cavalry skills were obligated to take lessons from this famous master.

The Duke of Newcastle stated that de la Broue cultivated his lessons to such a high degree of perfection that he must be quite accomplished in this profession in order to put them into practice. Even though this praise is a bit critical, it nonetheless gives proof of this author's excellence.

The Duke of Newcastle was an English nobleman and a governor to Charles II [1630-1685]. He honored the profession immensely by the unprecedented study he made during the course of his life, and he was also considered to be the most knowledgeable horseman of his time. We have from him two excellent books. One is written in French [*Methode et Invention Nouvelle de Dresser les Chevaux*, 1657 (*A New Method to Dress Horses*, Xenophon Press 2015)], was printed in Anvers, and contains many prints; however, since he had only fifty copies printed, which were presented to several princes and noblemen, and because he had the plates destroyed, the book is so rare that it is very difficult to find. The second work [*A New Method and Extraordinary Invention to Dress Horses and work them according to nature...*, 1667] is printed in English and was translated by Jacques Labassée de Soleysel, the author of *Parfait Marechal*.

Other authors, as many French as Italian and German, also wrote about the art of riding. However, some, because they feared being superfluous, so largely abbreviated their works that there is no adequate explanation of the subject matter; and the boring dissertation of the others, under a pretentious and improper scholarship, stifles the simple truth that is the reader's only interest.

Thus, properly speaking, the two authors I have just mentioned are the only ones who may serve as models. This is why, given the prospect of composing a systematic work based on sound principles, I have taken from both the most instructive parts, which will, at the same time, make a case in point for these two excellent men, whose memory could never be overly respected. However, to most readers, these works represent an impregnable treasure chest, either because they lack order or because they are filled with repetition. If possible, I hope to avoid similar criticism by developing my ideas in a precise manner and by adding to their clarity with the help of the diagrams found throughout this book.

The opinion of those who feel that there is no need for theory in the art of riding will not prevent me, in any way, from supporting it as one of the most important necessities for the attainment of perfection. Without the theory, the practice will always be uncertain. I admit that in a discipline where the body plays such an important part, practice must be inseparable from theory, because it is the practice that makes us begin to perceive the horse's temperament, natural tendencies, and strengths; and it is through this means that we discover his resources and his kindness that are buried, so to speak, in the quiescence of his limbs. However, in order to attain excellence in this art, it is necessary to be prepared for the difficulties encountered in the practice by a clear and firm theory.

Theory teaches us to base our work on sound principles, and these principles, rather than being opposed to what is natural, must serve to perfect nature with the aid of art.

Practice gives us the ability to easily apply what we have learned in theory. In order to attain this facility, one must like horses, be energetic and bold, and have abundant patience. Herein are the principal qualities of the true horseman.

There are few people who do not like horses. It seems that this tendency is based on the recognition we owe to an animal who serves us in so many ways; and if there is a person who thinks otherwise, he is punished for his indifference by exposing himself to accidents or lack of the usual aid expected from the horse.

When I say that it is necessary to be energetic and bold, I am not advocating violence and recklessness, which many riders boast of and which makes them undergo such great dangers, destroying the horse's spirit and keeping him in continual confusion. Rather, I am speaking of a supple strength that maintains the horse's fear of and submission to the rider's aids and punishments, and also conserves the ease, balance, and grace that are the properties of the good horseman and the result of an extensive progressive study of the science.

The difficulties involved in acquiring these qualities and the time required for achieving perfection in this work make many people, who assume an air of expertise, say that the *manège* is a worthless pursuit that ruins horses and only serves to teach them to leap and dance, thereby making them incapable of ordinary use. The consequence of this false prejudice is that there are innumerable people who disregard so noble and useful a discipline whose sole purpose is to supple the horses, make them gentle and obedient, and place their weight on their haunches, without which any horse, be he a charger, hunter, or school horse, could not be pleasing in his movements or comfortable when ridden. Therefore, inasmuch as the opinions of these people are without basis, it would be wasting energy to contradict these opinions that will destroy themselves well enough.

CHAPTER II

The Different Temperaments in Horses; the Cause of Their Indocility & the Vices That Result

An understanding of a horse's nature is one of the first basics in the art of riding, and all horsemen must make this their principal consideration. This understanding is only achieved through much experience, which teaches us how to explain the source of this animal's good and bad tendencies. When the proper stature and proportion of the parts is accompanied by a supple strength, and when one also finds in a horse courage, docility, and willingness, one can use these positive qualities to easily put the true principles of the good school into practice. However, when the nature is rebellious and one is not able to define the source of this obstinacy, one runs the risk of using methods that are more likely to produce new vices than to correct those one thinks one understands.

Unwillingness in horses ordinarily results from two causes: either exterior faults or those that are interior. By exterior faults, I mean weakness of the members, be it natural or accidental, which is found in the loins, haunches, hocks, legs, feet, or eyes. Since we have sufficiently detailed all of these faults in the first part, we shall not repeat them here.

The interior faults, which are directly responsible for molding a horse's character, are timidity, cowardice, laziness, impatience, anger, and malice, to which may be added, bad habit.

Timid horses are those who are in continual fear of the aids and punishments and who become skittish at the rider's slightest movement. This natural timidity will only lead to an obedience that is uncertain, unsteady, sluggish, and delayed; and, if one fights these horses too often, they become completely nervous and distrustful.

Cowardice is a vice that makes horses fearful and without heart. One refers to all of these types of animals as *carognes.* [Italian] [A variant of *charogne,* literally "carrion," [literally 'dead flesh']. This cowardice totally degrades a horse and makes him incapable of any type of bold and vigorous obedience.

Laziness is the fault of those who are melancholy, sluggish, and, so to speak, bewildered. There are, nevertheless, certain horses whose strength is dulled by the stiffness of their members, and, by arousing them with appropriate punishment, they can become fine horses.

Impatience is caused by excessive natural sensitivity that makes a horse high-strung, determined, spirited, and restless. It is difficult to achieve a regular and calm gait with these horses, because their extreme restlessness keeps them in a continually agitated state and the rider in an uncomfortable seat.

Angry horses are those who take offense at the slightest punishment and are vindictive. These horses must be handled with more caution than others. However, when horses with this fault are also proud and bold, and one knows how to handle them properly, one may bring forth more from them than from those who are malicious and cowardly.

Malice constitutes another natural fault. The horses that are plagued by this vice resist because of pure unwillingness and will respond only reluctantly. There are some who appear to obey, as if defeated and exhausted, but this is done to escape the punishments of the school and, as soon as they have recovered to a small degree their strength and have caught their breath, they fight back even more strongly.

The bad habits certain horses acquired are not always a result of interior vices but are often the fault of those who have ridden them badly from the beginning; and, when these bad habits have been implanted, they are harder to correct than a bad disposition resulting from nature.

The different vices that we have just defined are the source of five main faults of dangerous consequence: the possibility of becoming skittish, vicious, stubborn, balky, or obstinate.

The skittish horse is one who is afraid of a certain object and absolutely refuses to approach it. This apprehension, which often is caused by a natural timidity, can also be caused by some sort of sight problem that makes the horse see objects in a distorted manner; more often, still, this occurs when the horse has been overly beaten, which means that the fear of the beating, added to the fear of the object, weakens the horse's vigor and courage. There are other horses who, after being left in the stable for a long time, are frightened and alarmed when they go outside for the first time; however, when this fear is not a result of any other cause, it will not last for long if the horses are not punished and if one patiently acquaints them with what frightens them.

The vicious horse is one who, when punished, is malicious enough to bite, kick, and hate man. These faults are developed by angry and vindictive horses who have been unfairly beaten; for the ignorance and bad temper of certain riders produces more vicious horses than does nature.

The stubborn horse is one who resists out of pure malice and who refuses to obey and aid, be it to go forward, to back up, or to turn. Some have become stubborn because they have been overly beaten and restrained; and others, because they have been spared punishment by a rider who was fearful of them. Overly sensitive horses that resist fall into the category of this last fault.

The balky horse is one who fights the spurs, resists them, refuses to move and kicks in place, and backs up or rears, instead of obeying the aids and moving forward. When a horse resists owing to cowardice, this is indicative of a *carogne,* and even though he may make great and furious leaps, it is more a sign of malice than of strength.

The obstinate horse is one who refuses to turn, more out of ignorance and lack of suppleness than out of malice. There are horses that become obstinate in one direction, even though they initially seemed supple and obedient on that side, because one has forced them to obey too soon and has gone from one lesson to the next too quickly. An injury to the sight or to some other part of the body can also make a horse obstinate, and even stubborn, on one side. The fault of obstinacy is different from that of stubbornness in that the stubborn horse refuses to turn out of malice, even though he knows how to, whereas the obstinate horse does not turn at all because he is unable to do so, owing either to stiffness or ignorance.

When the faults we have just defined are a result of weakness and lack of heart, the horse's nature thus being defective and his essence being bad, it is difficult to compensate for this deficiency through use of the art.

The cause of the horse's defenses is not always found in his nature. One often demands things that the horses are not capable of doing in a desire to push them too fast and teach them too much. These excessive demands make them hate exercise, strains and tires their sinews and tendons, upon whose elasticity suppleness depends, and often these horses end up ruined when it is believed that they have been trained. Thus, no longer having the strength to fight back, they obey, but without grace or any spirit.

There is still another reason that contributes to the formation of these faults: the horses are ridden at too early an age, and because the work demanded of them exceeds their strength and they are not developed enough to resist the degree of control they are subjected to before being trained, their loins are strained, their hocks are weakened, and they are permanently damaged. The proper age for training a horse is six, seven, or eight, according to his native environment.

Rebelliousness and indocility, which are so natural, especially in young horses, are more developed in those horses who have become accustomed to the liberty allowed them in the breeding barn and following their mothers. They have trouble accepting the obedience demanded in the first lessons and yielding to the will of man who, taking advantage of the control he believes to have over them, overly exerts his domination.

This is accompanied by the fact that no animal better recalls the first improperly applied punishments than the horse.

There used to be persons in charge of exercising the foals outside the breeding barn when they were still wild. They were called *Cavalcadours de Bardelle.* Those with the most patience, skill, energy, and diligence were chosen; the perfection of these qualities was not as necessary for horses that were already being ridden. These people would accustom the young horses to allow someone to approach them in the stable, to pick up all four feet, to touch them, and to put on the bridle, saddle, crupper, girth, etc. They gave them assurance and made them gentle when mounted. They were never harsh or forceful, because at these times they would only use the gentlest methods that came to mind. Through this ingenious patience, they made a horse familiar with and a friend of man, maintained his vigor and courage, and made him understand and obey the first rules. If one were to imitate today the plan of these old connoisseurs, one would see fewer horses who are injured, ruined, one-sided, stiff, and vicious.

CHAPTER III

The Instruments Used in Training Horses

After the bridle and the saddle, which we already discussed in Chapters VI and VIII of Part One, the instruments used the most in training horses are the long whip, the switch, spurs, the longe, the martingale, the spike, blinders, the dock-piece, pillars, the leather cavesson, the iron cavesson, the bridoon, and the *filet*.

The long whip *(la chambrière)* is a strip of leather between five and six feet long, attached to the end of a fairly thick cane about four feet long. This instrument is used to animate and arouse a horse who is sluggish and resistant and as punishment for refusing to move forward. The long whip is also very useful for training a horse between the pillars; however, one must know how to use it correctly. The lash has been banned in all good riding academies because it can cause scars on the rump and belly; one must nevertheless sometimes resort to the lash in order to make a horse with a tough hide responsive and to make him fearful of punishment.

The switch *(la gaule)* is a birch rod that the rider holds in his right hand. It should only be about three and a half feet long, because if it were longer, its middle would come into contact with the shoulder, and it must be the point of the switch that makes contact. The switch gives much grace to a rider when he knows how to use it well, and it also shows the manner in which the sword should be carried on horseback.

The spur *(l'éperon)* is a piece of iron with three branches, two of which go around the heel. At the end of the neck, which is the third branch, there is a star that one calls *molette*\ it must have five or six points with which to prod or pinch the horse. The points of the rowels *(molettes)* should not be round and blunt out of fear that they could cause scars on the belly; on the other hand, they must not be too pointed, because this will distress a horse with a sensitive hide. The neck of the spur must be slightly long; otherwise, the horse would not feel the rowel as well, and the rider would be forced to move the leg too much in order to reach the belly.

The longe *(la longe)* is a long cord, about as thick as one's little finger, at the end of which is a buckle attached to a piece of leather that is passed through the middle ring on the iron cavesson. This instrument is excellent for accustoming young horses to trotting on circles with the aid of the long whip; it is also useful for those horses that are stubborn and resist out of malice or who are balky; the methods we shall explain in their appropriate place in the text.

The martingale *(la martingale)* is a leather strap, attached on one end to the girth underneath the horse's belly and on the other to the noseband by passing through the two front legs and running along the chest. Some riders try with this instrument to prevent a horse from fighting the hand and throwing his head; but this is a big mistake, because it confirms, rather than corrects, this vice. This invention should be banned from good riding academies.

The spike *(le poinçon)* is a wooden handle, from seven to eight inches long, with an iron point on the end. One holds the end of the spike in the palm of the right hand and presses the point on the horse's croup in order to make him stop kicking. I do not approve of this instrument at all because, aside from the awkward position of the rider's arm when pressing on the spike, there are two other inconveniences: either the point of the spike is so blunt that it has no effect or, if it is too sharp, it tears and bloodies the croup and makes long gashes on it. I prefer the invention of de la Broue, which is a type of spur neck with a rowel driven into it. This spur is attached to the end of a switch about two feet long such that it may be used as a switch carried in hand. The rider thus aids his horse with greater grace and ease, and does not run the risk of bloodying the croup.

Blinders *(les lunettes)* [or blinkers] are two leather straps that are put over a horse's eyes when he will not allow the rider to mount, tries to bite when the rider approaches him, or strikes at the rider with his front legs.

The dock-piece *(le troussequeue)* is a leather instrument, a good foot in length that is used around the tail of horses performing the high airs. This instrument is fastened by interlacing a strap through several small hooks. It is attached near the crupper loop by two small back-straps. At the base of the dock-piece are two leather reins, which pass along the horse's thighs and flanks up to the back-straps, where they serve to hold the tail in place. The dock-piece makes the horse appear to have a larger croup, makes him more graceful when performing the high airs, and also prevents the tail from getting into the rider's eyes.

Pillars *(les piliers)* are two round pieces of wood, each having a top, which are set in the *manège* about five feet apart. They must be six feet tall. Each pillar has different holes at specified distances for horses of different heights; or else, iron rings are placed on the pillars, and the cavesson ropes are passed through and attached to them. The pillars are used to accustom a horse to fearing punishment by the long whip, to animate him, and to teach him to piaffe and to raise his forehand. The pillars are also generally used in the academies for the horses destined to perform the high airs.

The leather cavesson *(le caveçon de cuir)* is a type of crown-piece made of thick, flat leather, which is placed on the horse's head and has two rope reins on either side to tie the horse to the pillars. A cavesson must be padded on the top of the crown-piece so that there is no chance of hurting the horse on the top of his head near the ears. Padding is also used on the noseband, which is placed above the horse's nose so that this part is not rubbed when the horse moves in the ropes.

The iron cavesson *(le caveçon de fer)* is an iron band shaped in an arc, with three rings attached, and mounted on a crown-piece and throat latch. Some are twisted, sharp, or flat. The flat cavessons are the best, because the sharp ones, which are hollowed in the middle and notched on the sides, rub the horse's nose unless one has them lined with leather. The cavesson should be placed a finger's width higher than the eye of the bridle shank, so that it does not hinder the action of the bit or the effect of the curb.

De la Broue, and after him the Duke of Newcastle, attribute such large benefits to the cavesson that I feel myself obligated to give an account here of what each of them has said.

De la Broue states,

"that the cavesson was invented in order to collect, elevate, lighten, teach turning and halting, stabilize the head and croup without hurting the mouth or the chin; also, to lighten the shoulders, front legs and feet, and to cure the faults of those trained horses who misbehave in the School, because the inside of the mouth where the bit comes into the most contact is more sensitive than the part of the nose where the cavesson is placed, and, in removing the cavesson, the horse is more attentive to the effects of the bridle and, as a result, lighter."

The opinion of the Duke of Newcastle is as follows:

"The purpose of the cavesson is to collect, elevate, lighten, teach turning and stopping, supple the neck, confirm the mouth, place the head and croup, keep the mouth sound and whole (as well as the bars and the part where the curb is placed), bend the shoulders, make them and the horse's forearms and legs supple, bend the neck and make it supple. A horse will then go better after the cavesson has been removed and will be attentive to all movements of the hand. It is not necessary to do everything with the cavesson, but the bridle hand must act before the cavesson, which is only an aid to the bridle.

"The longe on the inside of the cavesson, attached to the pommel of the saddle, gives the horse a nice bend, assures and subjects him to a true contact with the hand, and makes him firm on his haunches, especially a horse who pulls or is heavy on the hand, because it prevents him from leaning on the bit.

"With the cavesson pressing equally on the entire middle of the nose, one has a firmer hold to give a greater bend and to make the horse turn, the cavesson acting as strongly on the shoulders.

"A horse trained without a cavesson will never have that pleasing contact that all fine horses must have, which is to be even, steady, and light.

"The bridle shanks take longer to act and are so low that there is not enough room left, as with the cavesson, in which to draw them back. The bridle can, with great difficulty, draw the muzzle back.

"The cavesson and the bridle are very different in their effects, owing to the difference between the mouth and the nose. If you draw the cavesson upwards with your fingernails turned forward, this will raise the horse's head; and if you draw the bridle back with your fingernails up, this will only lower the horse's nose, especially if you keep the bridle hand low.

"When working only with the bridle, one can easily make mistakes, unless one is very knowledgeable of the different effects of the different movements of the bridle hand. One must thus necessarily want to be self-deluded if one does not wish to follow so short and sure a route as that of the cavesson attached to the pommel and supported by the bridle."

Considering the opinion of these two great Masters regarding the advantages and the effects of the cavesson, it would be rash not to follow so respectable an assessment. The only remark I shall make with respect to this is that I believe the cavesson to be excellent in the hands of a horseman who knows how to use it properly; but, at the same time, I believe that it is dangerous to give it to students, because our experience has shown us that those who have been educated in Schools where this instrument is used generally have a rigid, improperly placed hand, which is caused by the great force used in working the cavesson.

The bridoon *(le bridon)* is a mouthpiece mounted on a crown-piece without a noseband. It is a light, iron mouthpiece, broken in the middle; some are broken in several places. The bridoon is no more than an imitation of the first bridles that were used for riding horses and that consisted of only a simple mouthpiece without shanks or a curb.

There are two types of bridoons: one, which has a very thin mouthpiece, is used with a bridle and serves to lighten the horse's mouth; and, in the case of an accident, when the reins have broken, for example, or have been cut in combat, one may thus resort to the bridoon.

The other type of bridoon is the one used in starting young horses. The mouthpiece is thicker, and at the two ends are two small, round iron bars that prevent it from coming out of either side of the mouth when one of the two reins is drawn back.

Here is how the Duke of Newcastle explains the effects of the bridoon:

> "The bridoon only comes into contact with the lips and to a small degree with the bars, while the chin remains completely unaffected. It is good for elevating horses that lean on the hand, carry themselves on the forehand, and brace against themselves. One can reprimand a horse by firmly pulling on one and then the other of the bridoon reins, several times, as if one would like to saw on his mouth. It is also good for starting a young horse, teaching him to turn at the walk and trot, and stopping him: the constraint of the bridle [curb bit] can give the horse cause to fight back, and the bridoon prepares him to be more obedient to the bridle. It is necessary to have the fingernails down and to move the hands and arms forward. The bridoon is not good for those horses that have no feel and fight the hand, because while it lessens the feel of those who have too much, it spoils those who have none at all."

The filet[4] *(le filet)* is a type of bit, mounted on a crown-piece without a noseband, with a curb chain and shanks without chainlettes[5]. This bit is used for carriage horses or others when they are being curried or taken for a drink.

The English, who are more attentive than any other nation to a

---

4   No translation was given for *filet*, because its modern-day meaning, "snaffle" or "snaffle bridle," does not correspond to the definition given by de la Guérinière. His description of *the filet* invented by the English is probably what we now call a Pelham, and his explanation of the second type of bridoon is probably what we now call a snaffle or snaffle bridle. When "bridle" is used in this text, I believe it specifically refers to a bridle with a bit having a curb and shanks. When used with the first type of bridoon as described by de la Guérinière, it is what we now call a double bridle.

5   Small chains used to connect the bottom ends of the branches of the curb bit.

horse's equipment, have invented a *filet* of a rather unique structure. It serves as both the bridoon and the bridle [curb] at the same time by means of two pairs of reins, one of which is attached to the bottom of the shanks as in ordinary bridles. The other reins are attached to the two arcs that are at the two ends of the mouthpiece and, by using these two reins (the curb thus no longer acting), the mouthpiece acts like that of the bridoon and produces the same effect.

CHAPTER IV

The Terms of the Art

Nothing contributes more to the understanding of an art or science than knowledge of its special vocabulary. This is especially true for horsemanship, and that is why I have sought to give clear and precise definitions.

Manège [School] *(manège).* This word has two meanings, the place where one works horses and the exercises one has them do (school and schooling). There are both covered and open schools. A good covered school should be thirty-five to thirty-six feet wide and three times as long.

An open school can be wider and longer according to the terrain available, and it should be surrounded by a railing.

"*Manège*" as the exercises one asks the horse to do is the process of training him in all sorts of airs.

An air *(air)* is the graceful posture a horse should have at the various gaits. It is also the appropriate cadence for each movement within each gait, whether the gait is natural or artificial, which we shall explain later.

The change of hand *(changer de main)* is the action of a horse's legs when he changes his legs to *galop* [canter] on the right or the left lead. This term comes from the old Masters, who named the parts of the horse's body, rather than as other animals, as those of man's; even today, just as one speaks of the horse's mouth, his chin, and his forearm, one calls the horse's foot his hand.[6] Thus, to change the hand is to change the foot [leading foot, or lead]. According to custom, the change of hand

---

6   The "*hand*"—left or right—on which we work horses, refers to the horse's inside *forefoot* or *forehand*, and not the rider's inside *hand*. - Editor's note.

has also come to be understood as the path or track a horse takes when crossing the school before making a change of foot.

A track *(piste)* is the path described by the horse's four feet as he moves. A horse moves on one track or on two tracks. On one track, he goes forward in a straight line, his hind legs following the same line as his forelegs. On two tracks, the horse moves sideways, and his hind legs describe a line different from that of the forelegs: this is called *"fuir les talons"* [literally, fleeing the (rider's) heels; two tracking, moving away from the leg].

Aids *(aides)* are the means a rider uses to make his horse move and to guide him. These means consist of different movements of the hand and the legs.

Fine aids *(aides fines)*. One says a rider has fine aids when his movements are barely perceptible and when remaining precisely balanced, he aids his horse with skill, ease, and grace; we also call these "secret aids" *(aides secrettes)*. One says a horse has fine aids when he promptly and easily obeys the slightest movement of the rider's hand and legs.

Giving the reins, or yielding the hand *(rendre la main)* is the lowering of the bridle hand to reduce or eliminate the pressure of the bit on the bars [of the horse's mouth.] We must mention that the rider's left hand is always called the bridle hand, for even though the right hand is sometimes used to control the right rein, it is still only to assist the left hand, which always remains the bridle hand. [De la Guérinière's students' right hands had to be free to accommodate a sword.]

Hard, unyielding hands *(s'attacher à la main)*. This is when a rider has a rude hand and holds the reins more firmly than he should. It is the worst fault one can have on horseback, for this hardness of hand spoils the horse's mouth, accustoms him to rearing, and puts him in danger of falling over backwards, a quite deadly accident that often results in the rider's death.

Pulling on the hand *(tirer à la main)*. This is a fault of a horse that uses his mouth in opposition to the rider's hand by pulling, and raising his nose, either out of ignorance or disobedience.

Leaning on the hand *(peser à la main)* is when the horse supports his head on the bit and is heavy on the bridle hand so that, in effect, the rider must carry the horse's head.

Fighting the hand *(batre à la main)*. This is a fault of a horse whose head is unsteady and whose mouth is not made. To avoid subjection to the bit, he shakes the bridle and tosses his head up and down.

Crossing the jaw *(faire les forces)* is a very disagreeable habit of some horses. With an open mouth, they continuously move the lower jaw from side to side. It is a fault of a weak mouth.

Contact *(appui)* is the feel produced by the action of the bridle in the rider's hand and, reciprocally, the action the rider's hand produces on the bars of the horse's mouth. There are horses with no contact, others with too much, and others who are fully on the bit. Those who have no contact fear the bit and cannot suffer its contact on their bars, which makes them fight the hand and toss their heads. The horses with too much contact lean heavily on the hand. The horses with the best mouths have a contact on the bit; without leaning on or fighting the hand, they have a consistent, light, and moderate contact. These three qualities of a good mouth in a horse correspond to those of a rider's hand, which must be light, gentle, and consistent.

Halt *(parade)* is the manner of stopping a horse at the end of a lesson, thus *parer* means to halt.

Reprise is a repetition of a lesson, and during the interval between lessons, one lets the horse catch his breath.

(Marquer-un-demi-arrêt), to indicate a half-halt one holds the bridle hand close to one's body to retain and support the forehand of a horse that leans on his jaws, or when one wants to lower the horse's head [*ramener*] or to put him together [*rassembler*].

(Ramener) To lower the head and nose of horse's that pulls on the hand and carries his nose too high.

(Rassembler) To put a horse together; to shorten his gait or his air in order to put him on his haunches. It is done by holding the forehand gently with the bridle hand and driving the haunches underneath the horse with the calves. It prepares the horse to be put between the hand and the legs.

(être dans la main et dans les talons) To be between the hand and the legs is the quality of a perfectly trained horse who follows the hands, legs, and spurs freely and obediently, whether asked to go forward, backward, to one side or the other, or to work in one place. Such a horse submits to the legs and even the spurs without bending incorrectly or displacing his head. If one were to find such a horse today, one could, without pretension, give him the name, "Phoenix."

(Renfermer) To collect is to put a horse very much together, one who is advanced enough to start to come between the hand and the legs.

A horse is "well trained" *(bien mis)* when he is well put between the hand and the legs.

(Se traverser) occurs when the croup deviates from the path it should follow, either while going on two tracks or going straight.

(S'entabler) A horse may try to evade two-track work by going backward rather than forward, the haunches going before the shoulders. This term is seldom used any more, *d'aculer* having taken its place.

Harper. This is the gait of a horse with bone spavins that moves his haunches hurriedly instead of bending from the hocks.

Piaffe (piaffer) is the action of a horse who executes a passage in one spot, gracefully bending his forearms and lifting his legs without bending incorrectly, moving forward, nor moving backward, and remaining obedient to the rider's hand and legs.

Stamping *(trépigner)* is a fault of horses that piaffe badly, who in place of sustaining the elevated leg hurry their movement and stamp the ground. High-spirited horses are subject to this fault.

Turn across the school *(doubler)*. There is a wide *doubler* and a narrow *doubler*. In the wide *doubler*, one turns the horse towards the middle of the *manège* without changing the hand, dividing the *manège* equally. In the narrow *doubler*, one turns within a small square in the corner of the *manège*.

Falquer, falcade is the action made by the horse coming to a halt from the canter, his haunches showing a flowing motion, lowered and united.

Tride is a word coined by de la Broue. He used it to express the quick, short, united movements of the horse's haunches as he engages them under himself. One says a horse has a *carierre tride* when he canters short and quickly from the haunches.

To finish a change of hand, or half-volte *(fermer, serrer une demi-volte)*, the horse must arrive on the track straight, on one track parallel to the wall, in order to retake the other hand.

Working from hand to hand *(travailler de la main a la main)*, one turns the horse from a track mainly with the hand, using very little leg. This is good for schooling a war horse.

Secourir is to aid the horse with the calves or the inside of the thighs when he wants to stop or slacken his pace.

Chevaler describes the motion of a horse's legs as he moves on two tracks, moving away from the rider's legs, the horse's outside legs cross in front of his inside legs.

Inside and outside *(dedans et dehors)*. This is a manner of speaking used sometimes instead of right and left to express the aids one must give with the reins, legs, and heels, and also the movements of the horse's legs according to which hand he is working on.

To better understand this, one must know that the old Masters worked their horses almost always on circles, and the center around which they turned determined which hand they were on. When riding on a circle to the right, the rein, the leg and heel of the rider, and the horse's legs that were toward the center were called the inside rein, the inside leg, the inside heel; this is the same as saying the right rein, the right leg, etc. The outside rein and the outside leg are the left rein and left leg. Similarly, when riding on a circle to the left, the rein and the leg toward the center are called the inside rein and leg and are the left rein and leg, and consequently the outside rein and the outside leg are the right rein and right leg.

Since today the schools are rectangular and bordered by walls or rails, it is easy to understand what one means by the outside rein and the outside leg: those that are toward the wall. If the wall is to the left of the rider, he is working on the right hand, so the outside rein and leg are beside the wall and are the left rein and leg. If the wall is to the right of the rider, he is working on the left hand; the right rein and leg are the outside rein and leg, and consequently the left rein and leg are the inside ones.

I have been obliged to give these terms a rather overly thorough explanation because many people confuse them. But to speak more intelligibly, one says right and left, which is simpler, whether speaking of the rider's legs or those of the horse, and also the reins.

Regarding the terms that apply to the school airs, one will find explanations and definitions in Chapter V in the section dealing with the artificial movements.

CHAPTER V

The Different Movements of the Legs of the Horse and the Difference in Their Gaits

A good many riders who get on a horse do not have the slightest idea of how the animal moves its legs at the different gaits. An understanding of this is absolutely essential to the horseman. Without this basic knowledge, it is impossible to ever ride well.

Horses have two kinds of gaits known as the natural and the artificial. The natural gaits are divided into the perfect gaits, which are the walk, trot, and canter; and the imperfect or defective gaits which are the pace, a *traquenard* [a faulty trot in which the diagonal footfalls have become disassociated], and rack (*aubin*) [a broken gait of a horse between an amble and a canter.] Perfect gaits come wholly from nature, and are without the elaborations of art. Defective gaits are found in horses with natural weaknesses or in horses that are old and run down. Artificial gaits are those given by a skillful master to the horses he dresses [trains], in order to educate them to the different airs of which they are capable. These school airs can only be learned in a good riding academy.

Top: The walk.
Bottom: The trot.

FIRST ARTICLE: *The Natural Gaits*

The Walk

The walk has the least elevated, slowest, and gentlest action of all the gaits. In this movement, the horse lifts the two legs that are diagonally opposed, a foreleg and a hind leg. When for example, the right foreleg is off the ground and moving forward, the left hind leg is raised and follows the movement of the foreleg. The other pair of diagonally opposed legs move in the same manner. There are four movements in the walk. First that of the right foreleg, followed by the left hind leg to make the second movement. The third movement is that of the left foreleg, followed by the right hind leg, and so on, alternating between each pair of diagonals.

The Trot

A horse trots by lifting two diagonally opposite legs at the same time. Thus, his right foreleg moves with the left hind leg, followed by the left foreleg moving with the right hind leg. The difference between the walk and trot is that the trot is more energetic, active, and elevated. This is what makes the trot much rougher than the walk which is slow and close to the ground. There is also this difference between these gaits: it is that although the horse's legs moving in the walk will not be opposed and crossing [in diagonal pairs] as they are when trotting, the position of the footfall is known to be in four beat time in the walk, whereas there are only two beats in the trot, because the horse raises the two diagonally opposite legs at the same time and also sets them to the ground at the same time as we have already explained.

The Canter

The canter is the movement of a running horse. It is a kind of forward leap, because just when the forelegs are not quite back on the ground, and the hind legs are still raised, there is an almost imperceptible instant when all four legs are in the air.

There are two principal movements at the canter, one for the right hand, which is called cantering on the right lead. The other for the left hand, referred to as cantering on the left lead. In each of these movements the inside foreleg must advance and lead the way and the inside hind leg follows and advances too. This is done for each lead as follows:

When a horse is cantering to the right (on the right lead) and both forelegs are off the ground, the right forefoot is put down forward of the left forefoot. The right hind leg follows the motion of the right

Top: The canter disunited in front to the right.
Bottom: The canter disunited behind to the right.

Top: The unified canter to the right.
Bottom: Counter-canter to the right.

Top: The canter disunited in front to the left.
Bottom: The canter disunited behind to the left.

Top: *The united canter to the left.*
Bottom: *The counter canter to the left.*

foreleg; it also lands farther ahead than the left hind leg. In the canter to the left (on the left lead), the left foreleg leads, the left hind follows and lands farther ahead than the right hind leg. The order of the footfalls in these movements is as follows.

When cantering on the right lead, just after all four feet are off the ground, the left hind foot lands first. The right hind foot is put down next to make the second movement. It lands farther ahead than the left hind foot. At the same instant this right hind foot lands, the left forefoot is also put down, so that the two legs are diagonally opposed [united] as in the trot. A single beat is all that can usually be discerned by eye or ear. The third and last movement is marked by the right forefoot landing out in front of the left forefoot, and in line with the right hind foot. These movements are repeated at each stride.

On the left lead, the position of the feet is different. It is the right hind foot which marks the first beat. The left hind and right forefoot are raised and put down together as at the trot to mark the second beat. The third and last cadence is marked by the left forefoot, which lands ahead of the right forefoot and in line with the left hind foot.

When a horse is really supple, and able to get his powerful haunches well under him (*et le mouvement des hanches tride*), he marks cadence in four-time. When cantering on the right lead for example, this is done in the following order. The left hind foot marks the first beat. The second beat is the landing of the right hind foot. An instant after this, left forefoot marks the third beat. The right forefoot which is the most forward of all, completes the fourth and last beat. This renders a beat of 1, 2, 3, & 4; and constitutes the true cadence of a fine canter. This movement must be performed energetically from the haunches, but slowly and collected in front, as shall be explained in another chapter.

False and Disunited Canters

It sometimes happens that a horse does not observe the correct order of foot falls or the proper position of his feet as we have explained them for both right and left leads. In these instances, the horse is either performing a false canter, or a disunited canter.

The False Canter

In the false canter *(Counter Canter)* or the canter on the wrong lead, the horse leads with the outside foreleg instead of the inside foreleg as he should. This is to say, if while cantering to the right, the horse leads with his left forefoot, followed by the left hind foot. Then he is said to be false, the false canter, or that he is counter cantering, or that he is on the wrong lead or leg.

If when cantering to the left, he leads with the right forefoot instead of the left, he still remains false, on the false canter, or counter cantering or on the wrong lead. The reason for this is that when cantering on a circle, the inside fore and hind legs should be more ahead of those on the outside in order to better support the weight of both horse and rider, otherwise the horse would be in danger of falling while turning. This has happened more than once, and it is always dangerous. The rider takes the same risks when he allows his horse to canter disunited.

The Disunited Canter

A horse can perform a disunited canter *(Cross Canter)* in two ways: sometimes from the front end, and sometimes from the hind end. When disunited in front, the hind legs are moving in the correct order, but the outside foreleg is leading, instead of the inside foreleg. For example; when a horse is cantering to the right hand, and the left foreleg is leading instead of the right foreleg which should be more advanced, then he is disunited in front. When cantering to the left, if the right foreleg is leading instead of the left, the horse is still said to be disunited in front. It is more common to see the hind legs disunited. They are disunited in the same manner as the forelegs. If the outside hind leg is leading instead of the inside, then the horse is disunited behind.

In order to understand this best, remember that when a horse is cantering to the right hand, but has his forelegs placed as they ought to be when going to the left, then he is disunited in front. When the hind legs are in the proper position for the left lead, but he is going on the right hand, then he is disunited behind. The same holds true for the left hand.

In regard to hunters and hacks, the saying is heard everywhere, and certainly in France: "To canter on the good leg, use the right lead." Yet, there are some horsemen who pay no attention to this nonsense, but instead, change their horse's lead in order to rest the left leg which suffers the most [in the right lead canter] because it bears all the weight, while the right leading leg remains free in this work [on the right lead] and does not tire nearly as much.

ARTICLE II: *The Defective Gaits*

The Amble

The amble is a gait which is more extended and less elevated than the walk. It consists of two movements, one on each side. The fore and hind leg on the same side are simultaneously [or nearly simultaneously] raised, carried forward, and set down together. When they strike the ground, they are followed by the legs of the other side making the same movement which is continued, alternately from side to side.

Top: The amble.
Bottom: The aubin

For a horse to amble well, the haunches must be carried low and well bent. The hind feet should be carried a good foot past the forward hoof prints. This is how a good ambler covers ground. Horses that move with high stiff haunches do not move as well and tire the rider more. The ambler is at his best on soft level ground; a horse is not able to keep up this gait very long in mud, or over rugged terrain. Amblers are more often seen in England than in France because the ground there is softer, more level, and better suited to the gait.

Generally speaking an ambler does not last a long time. The gait is a sign of weakness in most horses that perform it. Young foals in the flat fields will amble until they have enough strength to trot and canter. There are fine horses, which after having given years of service, revert to the amble because their springs start to wear out and they are no longer able to maintain the other gaits which until then, were common and natural to them.

The Single-foot or Traguenard

The single-foot *(Entre-pas* or *Traguenard)* is a broken gait somewhat resembling the pace. Horses that have hardly any contact with the reins, are heavy on their shoulders, have legs that are used up or ruined, quite commonly will take on this gait. Cavalry horses, for example, that are obliged to work hard and carry heavy loads will, after several years of trotting, take to this hurried running kind of gait because they are no longer able to sustain the action of the trot. This gait has the air of the broken pace; it is properly speaking called 'the single-foot.'

The Aubin

The *Aubin* is a gait in which the horse canters with the forelegs while the hind legs trot or pace. It is an ugly, wretched gait found in horses with weak haunches and hind legs which have been ruined and in those horses that are extremely tired at the end of a long hunt. The majority of horses who prefer the *aubin* to the canter are, quite frankly, young horses with weak haunches that were started at the canter too soon and hunters whose hind legs are worn out.

ARTICLE III: *The Artificial Gaits*

Although the artificial movements are derived from the natural gaits, they take their names from the various cadences and postures which are taught to a horse in a school. A horse should be dressed in the school to which it is best suited.

In ordinary practice, there are two kinds of schools: schooling for war or cavalry training and schooling in the academy or *manège*.

In training for war, a horse is taught to be obedient and calm, quick on both hands, to make fast departs, to stop suddenly and turn easily on its haunches, to be accustomed to fire, to the noise of drums, trumpets, and cannons, to the flapping and waving of banners and flags, and not to be afraid of anything.

Schooling in the *manège* means performing all of the airs and figures invented by the masters who excel in this art.

These school figures are, or at least should be, practiced daily in good riding academies. Among these different school figures are the low and high airs. The low airs are those executed on the ground. The high airs are those movements of the horse performed above the ground.

The Low Airs or Figures on the Ground

The figures executed by a horse on the ground are: the passage, piaffe, *gallopade*, change of hand, volte, half-volte, passade, pirouette, and the *terre à terre*. Most of these terms are derived from Italian words because the Italians were the first inventors of the rules and principles of this art.

The Passage

Passage used to be spelled "*passege*" in French; this was closer to the original Italian word, "*Spasseggio*" which means to promenade. This gait is a walk or a trot, measured and cadenced.[7] In this movement the horse must prolong the time the legs are off the ground. A hind leg and a foreleg are diagonally opposed [paired] as in the ordinary trot, but the movement should be slower and much more sustained, collected, and brilliant. Forward movement is shortened so that there is no more than one foot of advancement for each step the horse takes. This is to say, the leg that is raised should land about one foot[8] ahead of the one that is still grounded.

---

7 Note that at the time, the passage could be a measured and cadenced walk or trot appropriate for a 'promenade.'-Editor's note.

8 *environs un pieds*-Note that the authors says "about one foot," which, at the time, the unit of one foot equalled 315.6mm or 12.45 inches.-Editor's note.

Top: The passage.
Bottom: The galopade.

The Piaffe

When a horse performs the passage in one spot without advancing, backing, or two-tracking, the movement is called the piaffe. The legs should be lifted high and bent gracefully. This gait, which is very noble, was in great demand in carousels and in riding exhibitions. It is still highly esteemed in Spain. The horses of that country, along with the Neopolitans, have a great deal of natural disposition for the gait.

The Galopade

The *galopade* or *manège* canter is a fluid, united canter, well-collected, shortened in the forehand, and diligent in the haunches. This is to say, a canter in which the hindquarters do not drag along and which by the horse's well-balanced, fluid movements produces that beautiful cadence which is a delight to the spectators and pleases the rider.

The Change of Hand

We said in the preceding chapter that a change of hand can mean not only a change of lead, but may also be used to describe the path a horse takes when going from one wall to another in the school, whether from left to right or right to left. In this last sense there are two forms to note. They are the counter change of hand and the reverse change of hand.

The counter change of hand is performed by leading the horse away from the wall and out toward the center of the school, just as one would in making a change of hand by going across it. But on reaching the middle, and after placing the horse's head in the correct position for the other hand, the horse is brought back to the wall it just left, continuing in the same direction that it was on before the change of hand [hence not changing direction.]

In the reverse change of hand the first path the horse takes is toward the center of the school, just as one would for an ordinary change of hand; once in the middle the horse is returned to the wall that he just left as in the counter change, but on reaching the wall the horse is turned, so as to reverse his shoulder and therefore his direction.

Thus, when changing from right to left in the counter change of hand, one finds himself on the same hand which is the right hand. In the reverse change of hand, on reaching the wall the horse is goes to the left by reversing his shoulder with a left turn.

The change of hand, the counter change of hand, and the reversed change of hand may be performed on one or two tracks, depending on the level of the horse's training.

Top: Volte to the right.
Bottom: Pirouette to the left.

The Volte

Volte is an Italian expression signifying a round or circular track. In Italy, *volte* means the circle described by a horse moving on a single track. Here in France, a *volte* is always performed as a two-track movement with the horse's fore and hind legs forming two concentric circles, or parallel lines if the *volte* is a square with rounded corners. What we call a *volte*, the Italians call "*radoppio*."

The half-*volte* is a half circle on two tracks. Half-*voltes* may be performed within a *volte* or at the ends of a straight line.

There are also reversed *voltes* and reversed half-*voltes*. By reversed *volte* is meant a horse moving on two tracks with his head toward the center of the circle. In this figure the forelegs are closer to the center and describe a smaller circle than the hind legs which are on the outside. This is the opposite of the ordinary *volte* in which the croup is toward the center. The reversed half-*volte* is made like the reversed change of hand, except that the horse must execute the turn on two tracks for the half-*volte*.

The Passade

In executing passades the horse is kept on a straight path, at each end of which it is turned from right to left and left to right in a series of half-*voltes*, each time passing over the same line.

Passades are performed in two ways: there is the restrained passade (*Passade au petit galop*) and the "*passade furieuse.*" In the restrained passade the horse is kept collected in a slow and measured canter. The cadence is maintained both on the straight line and during the half-voltes performed at each end. In the "*passade furieuse*" the horse is kept at a collected canter for half the length of the straight line and the last half of the line is performed at a full gallop at the end of which the horse is collected in order to begin the half-*voltes*.

The Pirouette

The pirouette is a kind of *volte* except that it is performed on one spot and does not exceed the length of the horse. The croup stays on the center and the inside hind leg serves as the pivot around which the horse turns, the forelegs moving much more than the outside hind leg.

The Terre à Terre

The Duke of Newcastle defined the *terre à terre* very well by describing it as a canter in two-time on two tracks. In this figure the horse raises both its forelegs at the same time; they are also put down together. The hind legs follow and accompany the movements of the forelegs. The cadence should be fluid and low, resembling a series of

Top: Pesade.
Bottom: Courbette.

low, short jumps close to the ground and always moving forward and sideways on the diagonal.

Although the *terre à terre* is properly classed with the low airs because it is a figure executed on the ground, it also serves as a basis for the high airs which are, like the *terre à terre,* performed in two-time.

The High Airs or Airs Above the Ground

The airs above the ground are all those executed more off the ground than the *terre à terre*. There are seven high airs: the pesade, *mézair*, courbette, croupade, ballotade, capriole, and the *pas-et-le-saut.*

The Pesade

The pesade is an air in which the horse's forequarters are raised high while remaining on one spot without advancing. The high legs are kept on the ground and do not move so that time is not kept with the haunches as is the case with all of the other high airs. This is a preparatory lesson useful for teaching a horse to jump easily and to control his forequarters[1].

The Mézair

Mézair means half air. It is a leap that is only a little higher than the *terre à terre*, but executed with less advancing. It is not as raised as the courbette. For this reason some riding masters call it a half courbette which is a good description of this figure.

The Courbette

The courbette is a leap in which the forehand is raised even more than in the *mézair*. It is also more energetic and sustained. The hind legs first bear the weight of the forehand and then accompany them, marking time with a low fluid cadence.

The Croupade

The croupade is a higher leap than the courbette. So much so that while the horse is off the ground, the hind legs are tucked up under the horse's belly at the same height as its forelegs.

Top: *Terre à Terre*
Bottom: *The Mézair*

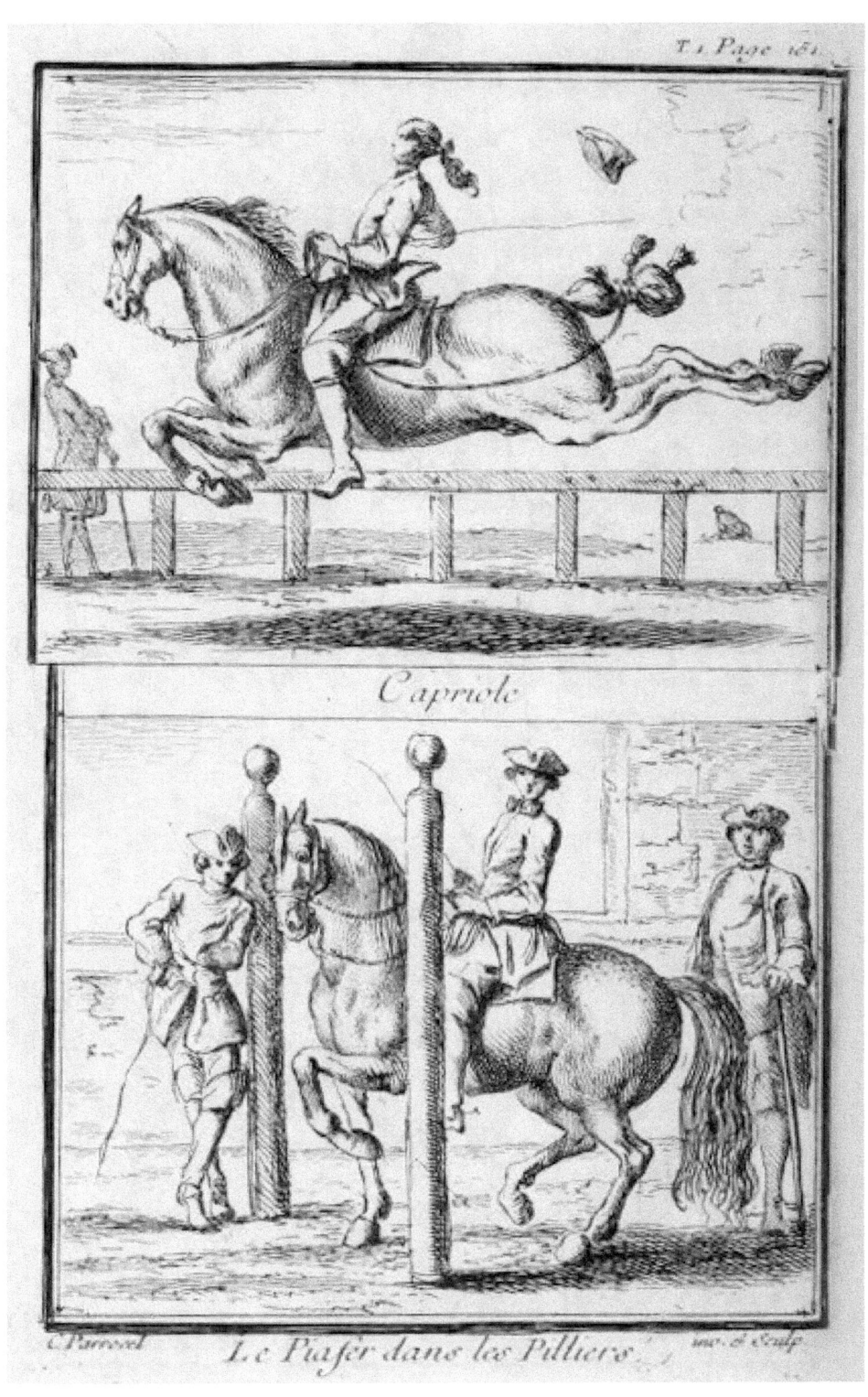

Top: *Capriole*
Bottom: *The piaffe in the pillars*

Top: Balotade
Bottom: Croupade

The Ballotade

The ballotade is similar to the croupade, but when all four legs are in the air and at the same height, instead of tucking them up under the belly as in the croupade, the horse shows his heels as though about to kick out, but without doing so as in the capriole.

The Capriole

The capriole is the highest and most perfect of all the leaps. When the horse is in the air and all four legs are at the same height from the ground, he kicks out with his hind legs. The kick should be executed with as much force as the horse can muster.

These last three airs: the croupade, ballotade, and capriole, differ in the following ways. In the croupade, when the horse has made his jump and is horizontal to the ground, he tucks his hind legs up under his belly. In the ballotade, the horse's shoes can be seen because he offers to kick out without actually doing so. In the capriole, the horse kicks out with as much force as he can.

The Pas & le Saut (The step and jump)

The step and jump is executed in three movements. The first is a collected canter or a *terre à terre;* the second, a courbette; and the third, a capriole. The three parts are then repeated. Horses not strong enough to perform consecutive caprioles take to this air on their own. Even the best jumpers resort to it when they tire in order to save themselves and to take the capriole with the best timing.

CHAPTER VI

*On Acquiring a Good Seat
& Things to Observe Before Mounting*

Gracefulness is such a fine ornament for a rider and, at the same time, such a great achievement in equestrian art that anyone who wants to become a horseman must, before doing anything else, take the necessary time to acquire this quality.

By gracefulness I mean an air of relaxed and easy competency that a rider must be able to maintain with correct posture and an independent seat in all of the movements that a horse is able to make.

This exacting balance depends on the rider's strict attention to the use of his body as a counterweight. Yet while doing so, his movements should be so subtle that they serve more to improve the appearance of his seat than to look like too obvious aids to the horse.

This fine point of the art has been neglected. Because of this, it is scarcely any wonder that horsemanship has lost some of its former luster. Carelessness and lack of concern have succeeded in occupying the attention that was formerly spent on acquiring and keeping the kind of seat that is a pleasure for spectators to see and which can add infinitely to the merits of an already beautiful horse.

Before mounting, the rider should check the horse's tack. This task, which takes just a moment, is absolutely necessary in order to avoid the possible inconveniences which might occur if attention to these small details were neglected.

First of all, see that the throat latch is not too tight, otherwise it would restrict the horse's breathing. For the noseband the opposite is the case, so check to make sure that it is not too loose. It should be kept a little tight to prevent the habit some horses have of keeping their mouths open. It also puts a stop to those whose fault is biting one's boot. After this, make sure that the bit is not so high as to wrinkle the horse's lips at the corners of his mouth nor should it be so low that it is carried against the teeth.

Make sure that the saddle is not so far forward as to hurt the horse's withers and hinder the movements of his shoulders. If the girths are too loose, the saddle will slide. If they are not well secured, it may fall off. This has been the cause of some unfortunate accidents. There are some malicious horses who inflate their bellies so much that one is scarcely able to bring the girths from one side of the animal to the other. There are others, who after being girthed and mounted, try to break the straps by jumping and rearing. In order to correct these faults, the horse should be saddled in his stall and then be trotted in hand for a few steps before mounting. See that the breastplate is above the shoulder joints; if it is too low, it hinders the movement. Finally, make sure that the crupper is the right length, not so long that the saddle can move forward nor so short that it chafes under the tail. This latter fault sometimes causes all sorts of unexpected jumping and kicking.

After completing this quick check, the rider should stand close to the horse's left shoulder. This not only makes mounting easier, but also helps to avoid being kicked, whether by a foreleg when standing too far forward or by a hind leg if too far back. The ends of the reins are now taken up by the right hand, checking to see that they lie flat. If they are twisted, they should be flattened by turning the bottom rein ring located at the base of the shank. The switch should now be transferred to the left hand along with the reins, leaving a little slack in them in case of accidents. With the same hand grasp a lock from the mane near the withers and keep a good grip on all three things.

Now take hold of the leathers, near the stirrup, with the right hand and turn them flat against the horse, then place the left foot in the stirrup. The right hand is placed on the cantle of the saddle. Then, rising straight up beside the saddle, swing the right leg over the horse, keeping it straight from the hip to the tip of the toe. The rider's body should be held upright while he is turning and seating himself in the saddle.

All of this which takes much longer to describe than to accomplish should be done with promptness, agility, and grace. The rider should avoid falling into the ways of certain horsemen who, perhaps because they do not see themselves while mounting, pay no attention to the deplorable figure they present while performing this simple but essential act.

When in the saddle, the switch must be passed tip up back to the right hand which also takes up the end of the reins in order to keep them at equal lengths. They are then adjusted in the left hand, using the little finger of that hand to keep them separated. The finger tips are now closed into the hollow of the hand, and the thumb is extended over the reins in order to hold them firm and to prevent them from slipping from the hand.

The bridle hand governs the horse's forehand. It should be held above the horse's neck neither to one side nor the other. It should be two fingers higher than the elbow and farther forward than the pommel of the saddle so that there are no obstructions to the effect of the reins. The bridle hand must be independent of the rider's body, kept at a distance from the stomach with the fingernails turned up a bit and facing his body. We shall discuss the effects of the bridle hand in greater detail in the next chapter. It is a subject that merits special attention.

When working with equal reins, the right hand should be carried close to and at the same height as the bridle hand. When turning with the right rein and using the right hand to do so, it should be lower and closer to the pommel of the saddle.

Immediately after adjusting the reins in the bridle hand and placing it correctly, the rider should seat himself in the middle of the saddle with his waist and buttocks forward so that he is not sitting anywhere near the back of the saddle; the reins should be held lightly but firmly to resist the horse's movements.

The Duke of Newcastle said that a rider's body should be two moveable parts and one which is immobile. The first of the two movable parts is the torso down to the waist; the other mobile part is the legs from the knee downward. Therefore, the immovable part of the body is from the waist to the knees. According to this rule, the moving parts above the waist are the head, shoulders, and arms. The head should be held straight and free above the shoulders, but relaxed, and should face between the horse's ears. The shoulders should be very free and brought slightly backwards; because if the head and shoulders were in front, the buttocks would be sent toward the back of the saddle. This is important because along with being very ungraceful, it also causes a horse to go on his shoulders and gives him that opportunity to kick or rush forward at the slightest movement from the rider. The arms should be bent at the elbow, joined with the torso without constraint, and fall naturally on the rider's hips.

The legs, which are the lower moving parts of the body, serve to guide and govern the body and hindquarters of the horse. When correctly positioned they should be straight and free from the knee down and close to the horse without touching his body. The thighs and calves should be turned in so that the flat portion of the inner thigh is glued onto the saddle flaps. Although the lower legs must be unconstrained and able to move freely, they must, at the same time, be secure and controlled. If the rider is not able to reliably control his legs, they will bang incessantly on the horse's sides, thereby keeping the animal in a state of continuous disorder.

If the rider's lower legs are too distant from the horse, he will not be able to aid or punish the horse when he should, which is at the time a fault is committed. If the legs are too far forward, they cannot be used on the horse's belly which is the correct place for the leg aids. If on the contrary his legs are too far back, the aids will be directed to the flanks, a part of the horse too sensitive and too easily punished too severely to apply the spurs there. One last point about the legs, if the rider's legs do not hang low enough when his weight is on the stirrups, he will push himself out of the saddle.

The heel should be a little lower than the toe, but not too much because that would cause the legs to become rigid. The heel should also be turned a little more in than out to guide the spurs easily and without constraint to that portion of the horse's belly which is just four fingers behind the girth. The tip of the foot should stick out of the stirrup about an inch, two inches at the most, depending on the width of the stirrup. If the toe is too far back, the heel is placed too close to the horse's belly causing the spur to constantly touch the skin. If on the contrary the foot is too far home in the stirrup, then the heel will also be too far forward, and the rider's legs will be prevented from correctly aiding his horse. Properly speaking, it is not the legs at all that need to be turned in toward the horse, but rather the rider's upper thighs. When the inner thighs are correctly placed, then the legs as well as the feet will be turned as much as they should be.

It is not enough to know merely how to sit a horse according to the rules we have given. The difficult thing is to keep this posture when the horse is in motion. It is for this reason that skillful riding masters, as a matter of course, require beginners to do a great deal of work at the trot until they are able to sit deep in the saddle. Nothing is better than the trot for giving a rider a firm seat. After this exercise, the other gaits which are less rough can be sat to without effort.

The old method of training the rider by requiring five or six months of trotting without stirrups is still an excellent system. By doing this, the legs have to fall naturally close to the horse. The rider also acquires a good seat and a sense of balance.

An error in training that occurs all too often is that beginners are put on *manège* horses to perform the high airs before they have gained a balanced seat at the trot. Correct balance is a far better method of riding than holding onto a horse with the strength of the legs. There are, however, riders who are in too much of a hurry to show on horses performing the high school airs. They almost always acquire the bad habit of holding onto the horse with their heels. This may do well enough in a school with trained horses, but when they leave the academy with their superficially correct seats, they often find themselves embarrassed by the antics of young horses.

It is only by progressing slowly by degrees that a rider can acquire the steady firmness and stability that comes from balance rather than from gripping with legs like steel clamps. This latter style of riding is best left to rough-riders and horse dealers. There are times, however, when the rider should use his legs, even forcefully at that, especially at the instant those sudden, unexpected incidents occur when he is not able to keep his seat, but must nevertheless remain in the saddle. The legs should, however, be relaxed as soon as the tempest subsides, otherwise the horse will begin its defense all over again and do an even better job of it than the first time.

After the work at the trot, the correct order of instruction in a good riding academy should be to put the rider on a horse between the pillars to perform the piaffe. He would be amazed to learn how easy it had become to ride this gait with good grace. After the piaffe, the rider should be placed on a horse who performs half courbettes. This should be followed by one for the courbette and then another for ballotades or croupades until finally he is able to sit to the capriole.

With this system of training the rider slowly but surely, without really being aware of his progress, acquires a good, firm seat without being stiff, inflexible, or cramped. He becomes free and at ease in the saddle without either neglecting the details that are required for a good seat or acquiring unnecessary affectations which would detract from his good posture. The most important thing of all is that the rider will never be off balance. This is the greatest of the faults a rider can commit because a sensitive horse will go either well or poorly, depending on whether or not the rider is in a state of continuous equilibrium with the moving horse.

CHAPTER VII

The Bridle Hand and Its Effects

The action of the bit in the horse's mouth is caused by the different movements of the rider's hand. These various movements of the bridle hand signal the rider's commands to the horse.

[Soloman] de la Broue, and after him the Duke of Newcastle have both said that a good bridle hand must be light, gentle, and firm. This kind of perfection comes not only from the action of the hand itself, but also from the rider's seat. When a rider loses his balance, his attention is concentrated on keeping his seat rather than on the effects of the bridle. The legs must also be used in conjunction with the hand; otherwise the effect of the bridle hand could never be just. This is known in the terms of the art as the harmony of hand and heels. This agreement of legs and hands is the combined perfection of all the aids.

The rider's hand must always begin the first effect; his legs then accompany the movement of the hand. This is a general principle that applies to the school airs, as well as to the natural gaits.

The horse has four principal movements. They are: going forward, backing, turning to the left, and turning to the right. The bridle hand must consequently also be able to produce four effects. These are: yielding, resisting, turning to the right, and turning to the left.

The first effect, yielding the hand, is used to move the horse forward. It is performed by lowering the hand and turning the fingernails downward a bit. The second movement, that of the resisting hand, is accomplished by drawing the bridle hand toward the stomach and turning the fingernails slightly upward. This aid is used to halt, to indicate a half-halt, or to back a horse. It is not really necessary to put much weight on the stirrups in order to properly perform this movement. The rider should, however, throw back his shoulders just a bit so that the horse will halt or rein back with his haunches under him. The third effect of the hand is the turn to the right. In this movement the hand is carried to the right with the nails turned upward a bit thereby permitting the outside, that is the left rein, to act. The fourth effect is the turn to the left. It is performed by carrying the hand to that side with the nails turned down in order to operate the outside rein, which in this case is the right rein. From what has been said so far, it is easy for the reader to see that a horse that is obedient to the hand is one who follows all of its movements and that the movements of the hand through the reins cause the bit to act in the horse's mouth.

There are three different ways to hold the reins:

(1) separated in two hands,

(2) at equal lengths in one hand,

or

(3) one rein shorter than the other [both reins held in one hand] depending on which direction the horse is worked.

The term "separated reins" is used when the rider holds the right rein in his right hand and the left rein in his left hand.

Separated reins are used for horses not yet accustomed to obeying the bridle hand. They are also used on horses that refuse to obey a signal to turn when it is indicated by the bridle hand alone.

In order to use separated reins well, the left hand should be lowered when drawing the right rein to signal a turn to the right. The same rule applies to the left turn. The right rein should be lowered when the left hand is drawn back because the horse would not know which hand to obey unless the hand opposite to the direction in which the rider wishes to turn is lowered.

Equal reins in the left hand are used to teach a horse obedience to the bridle hand. They are useful for the hack and hunter as well as for the charger, but when working with the *manège* horse, the inside rein should be held a little shorter in the bridle hand. This places the horse's head to the side toward which he is moving. The *manège* horse that is not bent has no grace at all, but the inner rein must never be too short; that would give a false bend and uneven contact. The rider must always be able to feel the effect of both reins in his bridle hand.

It is more difficult to bend a horse to the right not only because most horses are naturally stiff on that side, but also because of difficulties caused by the way the reins are held in the left hand. The left rein which is held under the little finger acts more powerfully than the right rein which is held above the little finger. When working a horse to the right, it is sometimes not enough to shorten the right rein to bend a horse in that direction. The rider is often obliged to operate the right rein by pulling on it with the little finger of the right hand. When used in this manner it serves the same function as the little finger of the left hand when working a horse to the left.

There are very few riders who know how to use the right rein really well. Most lower the left hand when drawing it back. The only thing they accomplish by this movement is to pull around the tip of the horse's nose because the outside rein is not able to sustain the action begun by the inside rein. Therefore when drawing in the right rein in order to bend a horse to the right, the feel of the outside rein must stay in the left hand so that the bend comes from the withers and not from the tip of the horse's nose, which is a very ugly movement.

The rider does not have this problem with the left hand. The way the rein is placed underneath the little finger makes it easy to bend a horse to that hand. Along with this, almost all horses find it easier to bend to the left. It should be mentioned that when a horse is well trained, the inner rein will need to be shortened scarcely at all and the rider, because of the harmony of his hands and legs, will only rarely have to use his right hand in order to bend his mount to the right; but until horse and rider have attained this degree of perfection, it will be necessary to use the reins in the manner we have described.

The height of the rider's hand usually regulates the height of the horse's head. This is why the hand should be held higher than usual for a horse that carries its head too low in order to raise it. The hand should be held lower and closer to the [rider's] stomach for the horse that carries its nose in the wind in order to bring down and lower its head.

The action of the curb is lessened when the rider moves his hand forward and consequently the effect of the bit on the bars is also lessened. This aid is used to urge forward the horse that holds back. We use this aid to drive forward a horse that holds back. On the contrary, a good method is if one holds the hand close to the stomach, with the curb placed a bit more firmly on the bars of the mouth, for horses that pull on the hand.

We have mentioned that a good hand combines three qualities: lightness, gentleness, and firmness.

The light hand is that which does not feel any contact at all of the bit on the bars.

The gentle hand is that which feels a little of the effect of the bit without giving too much contact.

The firm hand is one that holds the horse in full contact with the bit.

It is indeed a great art to know how and when to use these three different effects of the hand. Their use depends on the nature of the mouth of each particular horse. The effects must be applied without constraining the animal and without suddenly abandoning contact with its mouth. Stated another way, after yielding, which is the action of a light hand, the rider must gently take in the reins, looking for the feeling little by little, the contact with the bit in his hand. This is followed by the firm hand that resists more and more and keeps the horse in stronger contact. After this, contact with the bit is gently and gradually diminished before passing back to the light hand, for the gentle hand must always precede and follow the firm hand. The hand should never suddenly yield or resist. This can ruin a horse's mouth and cause head-tossing.

There are two ways to yield the hand. The first, which is the most common, is to lower the bridle hand in the manner already mentioned. The second is to take the reins in the right hand above the left and, by loosening the left hand, to gradually transfer contact with the bit to the right hand. Then the left hand is removed. After this, the right hand is lowered until it rests on the horse's neck. Then the horse is completely free and without bridle. This last method of yielding the hand is called *"descente de main."* It also may be performed by holding the end of the reins in the right hand at the same height as the horse's head with the right arm held straight out and forward. The rider should, however, be very sure of his horse's mouth and of its obedience before he attempts to try this last method.

The rider should guard against using the yielding hand or performing the *"descente de main"* when his horse is on its shoulders. The correct time to perform either of these movements is after indicating a half-halt. When the rider feels that his horse is on its haunches, then is the time to subtly yield the bridle hand or even to perform the *"descente de main."* As the rider abandons contact with the bit at the same time the horse is on his haunches, the horse has to become light in hand since he has nothing at all on which to support his head, This is one of the subtlest and most useful of all the aids in horsemanship. It is also one of the most difficult to know how to correctly time and perform.

There is still another way to use the reins, one that is not seen very often. This is to attach each rein to the saddle ring so that the curb will not have any effect. This method is known as "working with false reins." It is still sometimes used with young horses in order to accustom them to the feel of a bit when they are just beginning to be put in a bridle.

The Duke of Newcastle has done a dissertation on the bridle reins which appears to contain some validity in theory but which, in my opinion, does not hold true in practice. He states that "on whatever side the reins are drawn back, the bit always moves to the side of the mouth opposite the shank; that when the shank moves to the inside, the bit moves to the outside such that," as he continues to explain, "when the reins are held separately and the right rein is drawn back, the bit, as well as the curb, will act on the outside of the mouth, thereby making the horse look to the outside of the circle." This principle does not hold true in practice, which proves to us that the horse will always respond to the action of the hand on the side on which the rein is drawn back. For example, when the right rein is drawn back, the horse is obliged to give in to this movement of the hand by turning his head to the right. I will admit that, if one draws on the rein, without, as is necessary, bringing the hand back toward himself, contact will be greater on the opposite side; however, this will not prevent the horse from obeying the hand and turning his head to the proper side, because he is obliged to respond to the strongest signal. This does not come from the outside rein alone, but from the rein which, by activating the bit in the horse's mouth, draws the bit, and consequently, the horse's head, in the direction desired. In addition, by use of the hand at the proper moment, the inside rein is shortened slightly, thereby bringing the bit into contact with the part of the mouth one wants it to affect.

    It should be noted again that when using the outside rein by carrying the hand to the inside, that this action moves the horse's outside shoulder toward the inside. This causes the outside leg to pass over the inside leg. When the inside rein is used by carrying the hand to the outside, the movement will extend the inside shoulder. This is to say, make the inside leg cross over the outside leg. The reader can see that these different effects of the inside and outside rein are caused by the way the bridle hand is carried and that they are able to move the forehand of the horse. The rider who does not understand how to use the reins works without the aids of rules and basic principles.

CHAPTER VIII

The Aids and Punishments Required

to Train Horses

All animals as well as man are endowed with five senses. The rider must work with three of these in order to train a horse: sight, hearing, and touch.

A horse is trained through the sense of sight when he learns to approach objects that could frighten him, for no animal reacts more than the horse to impressions of objects that he has never seen before.

A horse is trained through his sense of hearing when he becomes accustomed to the noise of cannon, drums, and the other clamorous sounds of war. A horse should be attentive and obedient to the click of the rider's tongue. He should also respond to the sound of the switch and to the rider's voice which may at times be gentle when used to soothe; at other times a harsh tone may be required in order to threaten the horse. The sense of touch is the most important of all because it is through this sense that a horse is taught to obey the slightest movements of the rider's hand and legs. It is through touch that a horse acquires a sensitive mouth and sides if they are lacking, and it is through touch that these fine qualities are conserved in the horse that already has them. The rider uses aids and punishments to retain or to endow a horse with this sensitivity.

Aids are used to prevent faults that a horse might make. Punishments are used only at the time a fault is committed. A horse obeys through fear of punishment. The aids are nothing more than a warning to the horse that he will be punished if he does not respond to them.

The Aids

The aids consist of the different movements of the bridle hand, the click of the tongue, the whizzing sound and touch of the switch, the movements of the rider's thighs and calves, the gentle pinch of the spurs, and finally, the manner in which the rider shifts his weight in the stirrups.

In the preceding chapter we explained the different movements of the bridle hand and its effects. Now we shall go on to the other aids. The click of the tongue, a sound formed with the mouth barely open by curling the tip of the tongue toward the palate then quickly returning it, is used to wake up a horse, to keep a horse alert and to make him attentive to the aids or punishment which follow this sound. This aid should never be very loud. It should in fact only be heard by the horse. Worth mentioning in passing is that the click should never be used when on foot while a rider is near. It is a sign of rudeness and an offense against the horseman. It may be legitimately used when afoot on only one occasion that is at the time a horse for sale is being shown.

Although the switch is carried more for style than necessity, it nevertheless does sometimes prove to be a useful aid. It should be carried tip upward in the right hand in the same position a rider would use when carrying a sword.

The switch is at the same time both an aid and a punishment. It serves as an aid to enliven a horse when it is used to make a whizzing sound with the arm held high. It is also an aid when touched to the outside shoulder to raise the forehand. When the switch is carried tip downward and toward the croup, it serves as an aid to animate and enliven the action of the horse's hindquarters. It may also be used as an aid by a man on foot who can by touching it to the breast, raise the forequarters or by touching it to the knees, bend the forelegs.

It is incorrect to use a switch on a horse that is trained for war. These mounts must obey the bridle hand and legs alone when turning to either side or moving forward because the sword replaces the switch in the right hand. It is for this reason that the right arm is also called the sword arm. When working in a riding hall, the switch should always be held on the side opposite that toward which the horse is moving because it should only be used to animate those parts of the horse that are on the outside of the ring.

The rider has five aids in his legs. This is to say that the legs can make five movements, those of the thigh, the knee [or inner thigh], the calves, the pinch or the spur, and the shifting of weight in the stirrups.

The aid of the thighs and of the knees is done by either closing the thighs or the knees together tightening them toward the horse. This drives a horse forward; or one can tighten only the outside thigh or knee to impell the horse's inside hind; or one can squeeze only the inside thigh to support if the horse is pressing or hurrying too much on the inside. It should be mentioned that ticklish horses that resist and refuse to work through malice, will often respond more to the vigorous use of the thighs than to the spurs. Such horses may hold back for some time after being spurred but will set out willingly in response to the thighs.

The calves are used as an aid by bringing them gently against the horse's belly. This aid is used to warn a horse that he has not responded to the aid of the inner thighs and that the spurs are not far behind if he does not now pay attention to the calves. This aid is still one of the most gracious and useful that a horseman can employ to collect a trained horse. A sensitive horse will respond to the calves when the cadence of a school figure slackens.

The discreet and gentle pinch of the spur is an aid performed by subtly drawing the spur close to the belly hair without contacting or penetrating to the hide. It is a stronger aid than the thighs or calves. If a horse will not respond to any of these aids, then a brisk spurring should be used to punish his indocility.

The last leg aid, that of weighting the stirrups, is the gentlest of all. The rider's legs then act as counter-balances to realign the hindquarters and to keep the horse straightened between the heels. This aid presupposes that the horse is very obedient and extremely sensitive because it is the pressure alone of one stirrup weighted more than the other that the horse must interpret and obey. When the outside stirrup is weighted then the horse will quicken his action and move to the inside. When the inside stirrup is weighted then the horse is supported and restrained if he hurries too much. When both stirrups are pressed equally, the horse is given notice to pay more attention to his cadence and that he is holding back more than he should.

One should know better than to believe that this kind of sensitive mouth and sides can be maintained for long in horses left in a school. The different hands of various riders will cause them to lose the finesse and justness that are the special merits of a well-trained horse. The delicate sense of touch will also grow dull in time. But if training was based on sound principles, a good horseman can soon revive the merits that bad practices have destroyed.

The Punishments

The aids are only a warning to the horse that he will be punished if he does not respond to them. Punishment is consequently just the chastisement that must immediately follow disobedience to the aids.

It is very important that the degree of punishment should fit the temperament of each individual horse. Quite often the mildest chastisement administered justly and at the right time is sufficient to make a horse attentive and obedient. This method of using the mildest punishment required has the advantage of conserving both the good disposition and courage of a horse. A horse treated in this manner will progress further in his schooling than he would otherwise. The three instruments of punishment usually employed to correct a horse are the long whip, the switch, and the spurs.

The Long Whip

The long whip is the first correction that should be used on young horses. They learn to respect it when they are first trotted on the longe, which is also the first lesson that should be taught to a young horse. Another use of the long whip is to teach a horse to piaffe between the pillars. It is also used to make sluggish, lazy horses move forward; and it is absolutely essential for the restive horse that ignores the spurs. When properly applied, the long whip can make a greater impression on a malicious horse than those aids that only prick or tickle.

The Switch

The switch is used to correct a horse in two different ways. It is used behind the girth on the sides and the croup of a horse to drive him forward. The other use, a good smack on the shoulder, is just the thing to correct the horse that continuously bucks or kicks out of sheer malice. This punishment can be much more effective than the spurs because a horse cannot obey the spurs until he learns to understand and fear them.

Spurs

The spurs are an excellent remedy to make a horse keen and sensitive to the aids, but this form of punishment should only be administered by a wise and experienced horseman. It may be necessary to use them with force on occasion, but this should be done only rarely. For nothing is more likely to break a horse's spirit and drive it to desperation more quickly than spurs that are used too often and at the wrong times.

The spurs must be applied on the belly about four fingers behind the girth. If they are used too far back on the flanks, the horse will stop and kick instead of moving forward. If on the other hand the spur hits the girth, a fault of those who have short legs and turn their toes out, the punishment is useless since it has no effect.

In order to use the spurs well, the calves should first be pressed gently against the horse and then the spurs should make contact with the belly. Those riders who open their legs and suddenly slam the spurs into a horse surprise the animal and take it completely unawares. The horse is not able to respond as well as it might if it had been forewarned by a barely noticeable closing of the legs.

There are some riders who swing and bang their legs against the horse, thereby constantly jabbing the animal with their spurs. This causes a horse to incessantly whisk its tail while walking. This is a disagreeable habit in any mount, but especially so in one that is supposed to be trained.

Sharp spurs should not be used on horses that are restive and undisciplined. Such horses when spurred too briskly will piss with rage, throw themselves against the *manège* wall, or stop suddenly and lie down on the ground. Instead of curing these vices the rider will only create others. In order to accustom such horses to the spurs, they should only be applied after the long whip and at the time of a depart on either hand.

A gentle pinch of the spurs is an aid for some horses; for others that have very fine aids, even the most delicate touch of the spurs is a punishment. With such sensitive horses, a rider must be able to sit completely relaxed, without stiffness or rigidity, otherwise his mount will make sudden stops and plunging starts. This kind of horse reacts more to the subtlest touch of the spurs than a common horse does to a brisk spurring.

The horseman must thoroughly understand the nature of his mount in order to know how to make good use of the punishments. A horse should be chastised in proportion to the fault that he commits. The horseman must also know when to sustain, increase, lessen, or completely ease a punishment. He should furthermore not consider all of the faults that a horse commits to be vices because most of the time they stem from ignorance and often from physical weaknesses.

The rider must be able to aid and punish his mount without making excessive movements. A great deal of finesse and diligence are required because the correction must be administered at the very instant that a fault is committed. If the punishments are not used at just the right moment, they will prove to be more dangerous than useful. Above all else, a horse should never be chastised by a rider who is out of temper, angry, or enraged; always punish with equanimity.

It may truly be said that the proper use of aids and punishments is one of the finest attributes of a good horseman.

CHAPTER IX

*The Necessity of The Trot in Suppling Young Horses
& The Benefits of The Walk*

De la Broue could not give a more exact description of a well-dressed horse than by saying that he is the one who shows suppleness, obedience, and accuracy; the reason being that, if a horse's body is not completely free and supple, he will not be able to respond to man's demands with ease and with grace. Suppleness will always result in docility, because the horse will thus not have any problem in performing what is demanded of him: thus are the three essential qualities which comprise what is known as a *well-adjusted horse.*

The first of these qualities may only be achieved through the trot. This is the general consensus of all the knowledgeable masters, past as much as present, and if there are certain of the latter who would prefer, without any ground-work, to dispense with the trot and seek to develop this initial suppleness and freedom by use of a collected walk, they are wrong, because one can only develop these qualities by making the horse vigorously work all the parts of his body. This refinement results in dulling the horse's nature and in making him obedient in a lax, dull, and sluggish manner, qualities which are far removed from the true brilliance which is the ornament of the well-dressed horse.

It is through the trot, the most natural of all the gaits, that the horse is made light to the hand, without having his mouth spoiled, and stretches his limbs without risk of injury. This is because during this type of action, which is the most elevated of all the natural gaits, the horse's body is equally supported on two legs, one front and the other behind; this ensures that the other two legs, which are off the ground, may be easily elevated, sustained, and extended forward, thereby resulting in an initial degree of suppleness throughout the entire body.

The trot is thus, without question, the basis for all the lessons which contribute to making the horse skillful and obedient. However, although something may be excellent in principle, it must not be abused by trotting a horse for years, as used to be the practice in Italy, and still is in some countries where the Cavalry is otherwise quite well-respected. The reason for this is quite simple: the perfection of the trot, which comes from the force of the horse's limbs, that natural strength and energy which must absolutely be preserved in a horse, is buried and destroyed in the discouragement and weariness which results from an overly demanding and lengthy lesson. This problem is still experienced by those who trot their young horses on rough footing or in plowed fields. This is the cause of wind-puffs, curbs, spavins, and other hock ailments, all of which are the misfortune of those fine horses whose sinews and tendons are sprained by people who pride themselves in breaking a horse in a short period of time; such results in ruining rather than breaking them.

The longe, attached to the cavesson on the horse's nose, and the whip are the first and only instruments which must be used, on good footing, to teach the trot to young horses who have not yet been ridden or who have already been ridden but have misbehaved due to ignorance, malice, or stiffness.

When the horse is first trotted on the longe, he must always be put in a bridoon rather than a bridle. This is because a bit, no matter how mild it is, would injure the horse's mouth during those false or awkward movements usually made by young horses before they have acquired the initial degree of obedience demanded of them.

Assuming therefore that a horse is old enough to be ridden and has become sufficiently familiar with and quiet enough to allow someone to approach him and will tolerate the saddle and the mouthpiece, then the next step must be to put a cavesson on his nose, placing it high enough so it will not interfere with his breathing while trotting, and putting the noseband of the cavesson tight enough so that it will not move on his nose. The cavesson should still be lined with leather so that the skin on the nose, which is very tender in young horses, is protected.

There should be two people on the ground to conduct this lesson: one to hold the longe, the other to hold the whip. The one holding the longe must stay in the center of the circle on which the horse is trotted; and the one holding the whip will follow the horse and chase him forward with this instrument by giving some light taps on the croup and more frequent taps on the ground, because it is necessary to use punishment sparingly in the beginning so as not to discourage a horse who is not yet accustomed to it. Once the horse has obeyed three or four times in one direction, he is stopped and praised. This is done by shortening the longe little by little until the horse has arrived at the center where the person leading him is positioned. Then the person, holding the whip, hides it behind him out of the horse's view and praises the horse, this also being done by the person holding the longe.

After allowing the horse time to catch his breath, he should be made to trot in the other direction in the same manner. If a horse, as is often the case and not cause for alarm, canters instead of trotting, either due to good spirits or to a fear of the whip, one must try to discourage the canter by using the longe to lightly shake the cavesson on the horse's nose and, at the same time, by removing the whip from the horse's sight. If, however, the horse is stopping on his own and refusing to trot, one must use the whip on his croup and flanks until he moves forward. However, the whip must be used sparingly, because an overly frequent use of it will discourage the horse, make him vicious and an enemy of man and of the School, and will destroy his kindness which, once lost, will never return. Nor is it necessary (for the same reason) to make the lessons too long, because this will tire and bore the horse; rather, the horse should return to the stable with the same good spirit he had when he left it.

When the horse has begun to trot freely in both directions and has become accustomed to coming to the center, one must next teach him the change of hand. In order to do this, the person holding the longe must, while the horse is moving in one direction, back up two or three steps, pulling the horse's head toward him. At the same time, the person holding the whip must move toward the horse's outside shoulder and show him the whip so that he will turn in the opposite direction. He may even hit the horse if he refuses to obey. The horse is then brought to the center, is stopped, praised, and put back on the circle.

In order to make the lesson of trotting on the longe more profitable, attention must be given to pulling the horse's head to the inside by use of the longe, and, at the same time, to moving the horse's croup to the outside by use of the whip; in other words, pushing the croup to the outside so that it is moving on a larger circle than the shoulders. This enables the person holding the longe to pull the horse's outside shoulder toward the inside (the circular movement that the shoulder must make in this position, thereby suppling the horse).

After the horse has become accustomed to the obedience required in this first lesson, which will be established in a few days (if one follows the method we have just explained) he may then be ridden, taking all precautions necessary to keeping him quiet when being mounted. Once the rider is in the saddle, he must try to teach the horse the first principles related to an understanding of the hand and the legs, which is done in the following manner. The rider must hold the bridoon reins separated in both hands and, when he wants to make the horse walk, he will lower both his hands while lightly placing his calves near the horse's sides. Spurs should not be used, since they are not necessary in the beginning. If the horse does not respond to these initial aids, which oftentimes is the case because he does not understand them, the whip must be used, because the horse has already grown accustomed to moving away from it. The whip will thus serve as punishment when the horse does not want to move forward from the rider's legs; however, the whip should only be used when the horse refuses to obey the movements of the rider's thighs and calves.

Similarly, in order to teach the horse to turn from the hand, the rider must draw the inside bridoon rein back and, when the horse refuses to turn, the person holding the longe must, at the same time, pull on the head and make the horse turn. Just as the whip makes the horse move away from the leg, this will serve as the means for making the horse accustomed to turning from the hand until he finally becomes accustomed to following the rider's hand and moving away from the rider's legs. This will be accomplished in a short period of time if one uses the first aids with the judgement and discretion which are necessary in starting young horses; because it is the lack of care in the beginning which is the source of most of the vices and problems horses have in the future.

Once the horse has begun to obey with ease and to initiate a movement without hesitation, be it turning from the hand or moving forward from the leg and changing hand (all of which he has just learned), the next step is to determine what type of temperament he has in order that his trot may be adjusted to his disposition and his spirit.

In general, there are two types of temperaments in horses. There are those who hold themselves back and are usually light in the hand; and there are others who throw off all restraint and are, for the most part, heavy or pull on the hand.

In regard to those who naturally hold themselves back, they must be made to assume a bold, long-striding trot in order to loosen their shoulders and their haunches. As for the others, who are naturally heavy or pull on the hand with the nose held out, their trot must be more elevated and measured in order to prepare them for collection. However, both types must be kept at an even, steady trot and not allowed to drag their haunches, and the lesson must maintain the same degree of energy from start to finish without, however, its repetition being too lengthy.

The purpose of these first lessons should not be to make the horse's mouth nor should it be to stabilize his head. It is necessary to wait until the horse has become supple and able to easily turn in both directions. In this way, the horse's mouth will remain sensitive, and thus it is that the bridoon is excellent to use in the beginning, because it exerts very little pressure on the bars and practically no pressure on the chin, a very delicate part where, as the Duke of Newcastle explains so well, the true feeling of the horse's mouth is found.

Once the horse has begun to obey the hand and the legs, without the aid of the longe or whip, he should be taken, and not any too soon, off the longe and made to walk on a straight line; thus leaving the circle and squaring his body or, in other words, learning to move straight forward and to familiarize himself with the terrain. Once the horse is walking well on the four lines and in the four corners of the ring he has been put on, one must next make him trot on these same lines, with the bridoon reins still being held separately, such that the four sessions (which are sufficient for each day and each time the horse is ridden), consist of two at the walk and two at the trot, carried out alternately and ending with the trot, because this is the gait which will lead to the initial suppleness.

If the horse continues to easily obey at the walk and the trot in a bridoon, one may begin to use a bridle having a bit with a simple canon and a straight shank, as this is the first type of mouthpiece used on young horses.

The Walk

Even though I view the trot as the basis for the initial freedom one must give to horses, I do not mean by this to exclude the walk, which also has its own special value.

There are two types of walk: the *country walk* and the *school walk.*

A definition of the country walk has already been given in the chapter on the natural gaits, and we have said that its action is the least elevated and slowest of all the natural gaits, which makes it a smooth and comfortable gait. This is because, during this type of action, the horse stretches his legs forward and close to the ground, thus not shaking the rider as during the other gaits where, because the movements are more elevated and above the ground, the rider, unless he is quite accomplished, must continually concentrate on his posture.

The school walk differs from the country walk in that its action is more sustained, measured, and collected; this makes it very useful in making the horse's mouth, confirming his memory, re-establishing trust in his rider, and making him able to bear the pain and fear of the strict lessons which are necessary in order to supple and confirm him enough so that he will move in obedience to the hand and the legs. Thus are the benefits derived from the school walk. They are so great that there is no horse, regardless of his degree of training, that will not profit from this lesson.

However, because a young horse, who has just been worked at a long-striding trot, cannot as yet be made to shorten to a collected gait, like the school walk, I do not feel that he can be put under this sort of restriction until he has been properly prepared by use of halts and half-halts, which will be discussed in the next chapter.

Thus, a horse that is just learning the trot should be put in a slow, fairly long-striding walk, in order to give him some confidence and memory. However, as soon as he maintains freedom in his shoulders at the walk, he must be put on many straight lines from which he is turned sometimes to the right and sometimes to the left to establish a new line, the length depending upon whether he is holding back or moving forward too freely.

It is not necessary to turn the horse's entire body onto these different straight lines, but only his shoulders, always making him move forward after having turned. This manner of turning the shoulders onto many straight lines in both directions, without any observation of the terrain other than turning and going straight following the rider's will, is much better than putting the horse on a circle; because, following this method, the haunches are kept on the same line as the shoulders, and, on the circular line, the horse is inclined outside of the straight line. However, when the horse becomes stiff, hard, or resists in one direction, he must be returned to the circle. This is the only remedy; I also view it as a punishment. This is why I advise that any horse that resists during the beginning of his training be put back on the longe. This punishment has more effect and corrects a horse better than any scolding he may be given while at liberty.

Even though the lesson of putting the horse on new and frequent straight lines is excellent for teaching a horse to turn with ease, it is necessary, once he has become obedient during this lesson and once one wishes to use him for hacking, to put him on a single, long, straight line in order that he may develop a lengthened stride at the walk; and one must turn him only from time to time in order to maintain obedience to the hand and suppleness in the shoulders. However, for this the horse must be taken into the open country, because the footing in a school is not varied enough.

If one finds that the walk is not natural to a lazy and sluggish horse, because he is not yet supple enough, this horse must be made to assume a bold, vigorous trot and even punished with the spurs and the switch until he finally adopts a lively, animated walk.

CHAPTER X

On The Halt, The Half-Halt, & The Rein Back

After having shown, in the preceding chapter, that the trot is the only means of giving young horses the initial suppleness needed to prepare them to be obedient, it is necessary to move to another lesson, which is just as useful, because it consists of preparing them for placing their weight on their haunches which results in making them pleasing and light in the hand.

One refers to a horse as being on his haunches when he lowers his haunches and brings them underneath himself, while moving the back hooves and hocks forward under the belly. This is done to give the haunches a natural equilibrium to counterbalance the forehand which is the weakest part; it is from this equilibrium that a pleasing and light mouth is produced in the horse.

It must be noted that a horse, when moving, is naturally inclined to use the force of his loins, haunches, and hocks to thrust his entire body forward; and since his shoulders and forearms are being used to support this action, the horse is, out of necessity, on his shoulders and, consequently, heavy in the hand.

In order to place a horse on his haunches and cure him of the fault of being on his shoulders, horsemen have found a cure in the lessons of the halt, the half-halt, and the rein back.

On the Halt

The halt is the effect achieved by the action one makes in drawing the horse's head and the other parts of the forehand back with the bridle hand and, at the same time, in delicately driving the haunches forward with the calves, so that the horse's entire body is sustained in this equilibrium while remaining on his back legs and hooves. This action, which is very useful in making a horse light in the hand and pleasing to his rider, is much more difficult for the horse than that of turning, which is more natural to him.

In order to achieve a good halt, the horse must already have been slightly animated, and, when one feels that he has quickened the cadence of his pace, one must, by delicately rousing him with the calves, place the shoulders more and more to the rear and hold the bridle hand more and more firmly until the halt is formed: in other words, until the horse is completely stopped. While moving the body back, one must move the elbows slightly closer to the body in order to have more firmness in the bridle hand. It is also necessary that the horse remain straight in the halt, so that this action is achieved on the haunches; because, if one of the back legs is off the line of the shoulders, the horse moving sideways in this action, he cannot be on his haunches.

The advantages derived from a well executed halt are to collect a horse, steady his mouth, head, and haunches and to make him light in the hand. However, as beneficial as the halts may be when they are executed at the right moment, so may they be harmful when used improperly. In order to know when to use them, it is necessary to consider the horse's temperament, because the best lessons, which are only invented in order to perfect his temperament, would produce the opposite effect if one were to be abusive by exercising them inappropriately.

At the first sign of lightness in the trot and of ease in turning in either direction, one may begin to indicate the halts to a horse, but rarely before this point, by holding the horse little by little and gently; because a halt executed abruptly (as if, in one beat, one were to plant the horse on his hind-end) would weaken the horse's loins and hocks and could even disable a young horse who has not yet developed all of his strength.

Aside from the young horses, which must never be hurried or stopped too roughly, there are still others who must be halted with care, whether due to faulty build or to natural weakness; this we will examine.

1. Since the head is the first part which must be collected at the halt, if the horse has too narrow a jaw, he will have difficulty sustaining this action; likewise, if the neck and shoulders are poorly built and inverted, which is called *Encolure de Cerf* (neck and shoulders of a deer), he will stiffen himself and the halt will be rough and crooked; if the hooves are weak and sore, he will run away from the halt and he will be much more thrown on the forehand and on the bit than if the weakness were to come from the legs, the shoulders, or the haunches.

2. Horses that are long in the body and sore are usually weak in the loins and consequently form bad halts, due to the difficulty they have in bringing themselves together and back on their haunches. This causes several problems: either they refuse to move forward again after halting or they assume a kind of single-foot or rack or they throw themselves on the rider's hand to escape the restraint of a new halt.

3. Sway-backed horses, whose backs are weak and sunken, have difficulty in placing their heads at the halt; because the strength of the nape of the neck is dependent upon the strength of the loins, and when a horse is suffering from some soreness in these parts, he gives

evidence of this by an unpleasant action with his head.

4. Horses that are overly sensitive, impatient, and angry fight the least bit of constraint and consequently the halt, and their mouths are usually hard and unconfirmed; thus impatience and spirit destroys the memoryand the sensitivity in the mouth and makes the effects of the hand and the legs useless.

5. Finally, there are some horses who, although weak, stop short in order to avoid being halted by the rider, and since they are fearful of the surprise, they do not want to move forward again at all. Others, of the same temperament, fight the hand when they realize that one wants to halt them. Both must be halted rarely and when they are not anticipating it.

Thus, the halt is only good for horses that have strong loins and enough strength in the haunches and hocks to support this action. At the trot, the halt must be executed in a single beat, with the hind feet straight such that one is not farther forward than the other, and without crossing over, which results in the horse being supported equally on the haunches. However, at the canter, where the action is more lengthened than at the trot, the horse must be halted in two or three beats, when the front feet return to the ground, so that in elevating himself, he will be on his haunches. This is achieved by drawing the hand back, while aiding the horse slightly with the inner thighs or the calves, in order to make him throw himself on his haunches or slide his haunches underneath himself.

It must be noted that blind horses halt more easily than others because of their fear of taking a false step.

On the Half-Halt

The half-halt is the action one makes in holding the bridle hand close to oneself with the fingernails turned slightly up; rather than to completely halt the horse, it is used only to hold and support the forehand when the horse is leaning on the bit or else when one wants to *ramener* the horse [bring his head down and round the neck] or to *rassembler* the horse [bring him together or collect him].

We have said, above, that the halt is only suited to a very small number of horses, due to the fact that there are very few of them who would have enough strength in the loins and hocks to support this action.

Therefore the greatest proof of a horse's strengths and obedience is the execution of a light and steady halt after a last pace, which is rare since, to go so quickly from one extreme to the other, it is necessary that the horse have an excellent mouth and haunches. To the extent that these violent halts can ruin and discourage a horse, they are only used as a test.

Such is not the same case with the half-halt, where the horse is only held slightly more in hand without being completely halted. This action does not make the horse as anxious and stabilizes his head and haunches with less constraint than does the halt; it is for this reason that the half-halt is more useful forming the horse's mouth and achieving lightness. One can repeat the half-halt often without breaking the horse's gait; and since, through this aid, one brings the horse's head down and raises his forehand, one thus makes the horse lower his haunches at the same time, which is what is wanted.

The half-halt is thus suited to all types of horses, but there are certain temperaments with which it must be used sparingly. When, for example, a horse holds back on his own, one only indicates the half-halt when one wants him to accept more contact; and in order to prevent him from stopping completely by this movement, one aids him with the inner thighs, the calves, and sometimes the spurs, depending upon how much he is holding himself back. However, if the horse leans too heavily on the hand, the half-halts must be more frequent and only indicated by the bridle hand without any aid from the inner thigh or the legs; rather it is necessary to loosen the thighs or else he would throw himself on the forehand to an even greater degree.

When, in indicating a halt or a half-halt, the horse continues to lean on the bit, to pull at the hand, and even sometimes to force the hand by moving forward despite the rider's will, it is thus necessary, after having halted the horse, to back him up as punishment for this disobedience.

On the Rein Back

The position of the bridle hand, to back a horse, is the same as at the halt because in accustoming a horse to back up easily, it is necessary (after having halted him) to draw back on the bridle, with the fingernails up, as if one wished to indicate a new halt. When the horse obeys, which is to say that he takes one or two steps backwards, it is necessary to yield the hand so that the senses that cause the feeling return to the bars; otherwise this part would be made numb and insensitive, and the horse, instead of obeying and backing up, would force the hand or almost rear.

Even though the rein back is a punishment for a horse who does not obey the halt well, it is still a means of preparing him to place his weight on his haunches, to position his back feet, to steady his head, and to make him light in the hand.

When a horse backs up, one of his back legs is always under the stomach, he pushes the rump back, and he is, in every movement, sometimes on one haunch, sometimes on the other. However, he cannot accomplish this action well, and one must not demand it of him until he begins to supple himself and obey the halt; because it is easier to draw the forehand back to oneself when the shoulders are free rather than numb, and, since this lesson causes soreness in the loins and hocks, it is necessary to use it moderately in the beginning.

When a horse persists in not wanting to back at all, which happens to almost all the horses who have not once practiced this lesson, a person on foot lightly uses the point of the switch on the knees and the fetlocks, which are the two leg joints, in order to make the horse bend his leg; and, at the same time, the rider draws the bridle hand back toward himself, and, as soon as the horse obeys by taking a single step back, it is necessary to praise and caress him in order to make him know that this is what is demanded of him. After having made a difficult horse back up a few steps and after having praised him, one must then keep him slightly in hand (as if one wanted to back him up again), and, when one feels him lower his haunches in order to prepare himself to back up, it is necessary to halt him and praise him for this action which proves that he will soon back up at the rider's will.

In order to back a horse according to strict rule, it is necessary, during each step he takes back, that he remain ready to move forward again; it is a big mistake to rein back too quickly since the horse, thus accelerating his energies to the rear, could drive himself back and even be in danger of falling over, especially if he has weak loins. Moreover, it is necessary that he backs up on a straight line, without moving sideways, so that both haunches are equally brought under him while backing.

When a horse begins to back up easily, the best lesson that one can give to make him light in the hand is to only rein back the shoulders; in other words, to gently bring the forehand back to oneself as if one wanted to back him, and when one feels that the horse will back, one must give him the reins and walk forward one or two steps.

After having halted or backed the horse, it is necessary to gently draw the horse's head to the inside in order to play with the bit in the mouth, which pleases the horse and accustoms him to bending in the direction that he is moving. This lesson prepares him also for that of the shoulder-in which we will speak about in the next chapter.

CHAPTER XI

On The Shoulder-In

We have already stated that the trot is the basis for the initial suppleness and obedience which must be given to horses; and this principle is generally accepted by all the skilled riding masters. However, this same trot, be it on a straight line or circles, only provides the horse's shoulder and leg with a forward movement when he goes on the straight line and a slightly circular movement of the outside shoulder and leg when he goes on the circle; but it does not provide a sufficient stepping over of the legs which is the action that a well dressed horse must perform who understands the heels and who, in other words, easily moves sideways in both directions.

In order to understand this properly, one must take note of the fact that a horse's legs have four movements. The first is that of the shoulder brought forward when it is moved directly in front of the horse. The second movement is that of the shoulder brought back when he backs up. The third movement is when the horse raises the leg and the shoulder in place, without moving forward or back, which is the action of the piaffe. And the fourth is the circular stepping-over movement which must be made by the horse's shoulder and leg when he turns sharply or moves sideways.

The first three movements are easily achieved through the trot, the halt, and the rein back. However, the last movement is the most difficult, because if, during this movement (where the horse must cross and *"chevaler"* the outside leg over the inside leg) the crossing of the leg is neither forward nor circular, the horse will catch his leg which is on the ground and supporting his weight, and the pain of the blow can cause him injury or, at the least, make him assume a false position; this often happens to horses who are not sufficiently supple in the shoulders. The difficulty in finding reliable rules for giving the shoulder and the leg ease in this circular movement of one leg over the other has always embarrassed [challenged] riders because, without this perfection, a horse cannot turn easily nor move sideways from the leg gracefully.

In order to thoroughly examine the lesson of the shoulder-in, which is the most difficult and the most useful of all those which must be used to supple the horse, it is necessary to examine what de la Broue and The Duke of Newcastle have said on the subject of the circle which, according to the latter, is the only means of perfectly suppling the horse's shoulders.

The shoulder-in [right]

De la Broue states that:

"not all horses' temperaments and dispositions are suited to this unusual constraint of always turning on circles to supple them; and since their strength is not capable of making so many revolutions all in one breath [in constant repetition], they are repelled [balk] and stiffen more and more instead of being suppled."

The Duke of Newcastle explains himself as follows:

"The head to the inside, the croup to the outside, on a circle, initially places the horse on the forehand; it takes support and softens the shoulders extremely, etc.

"Trotting and cantering with the head to the inside, the croup to the outside, makes the entire forehand move toward the center; and the hindend moves away from the center, being pressed more by the shoulders than by the croup.

"Anyone who tracks on a large circle works more, because he is making a greater path than someone who tracks on a smaller circle, having to make more movement and due to the necessity that the legs to be freer; the others [ones on the smaller circles] are more constrained and subjected on the smaller circle, because the forehand supports the entire body, whereas those that make the bigger circle are suspended for a longer time.

"The shoulder cannot become supple if the inside hind leg, when working, is not in front of and close to the outside hind leg."

One sees, through the very correct reasoning of these two great men, that both have acknowledged the circle, but de la Broue does not always make use of it and he often prefers the square.

As for the Duke of Newcastle, for whom the circle is the most preferred lesson, he himself admits to the inconveniences found with it when he says that, on the circle, with the head to the inside, the croup to the outside, the parts of the forehand are more subjected and constrained than those of the hind end and that this lesson places a horse on the forehand.

This acknowledgement, which experience confirms, clearly proves that the circle is not the true means of perfectly suppling the shoulders, since something which is constrained and burdened by its own weight cannot become light; however, a great truth acknowledged by this famous author is that the shoulder cannot be suppled if the inside hind leg, while moving, is not in front of, and close to the outside hind leg. It is this wise observation which made me seek and discover the lesson of the shoulder-in, which we will explain.

Thus, once a horse has learned to trot freely in both directions on the circle and on the straight line, to move at a calm and even walk on these same lines, has become accustomed to executing halts and half-halts

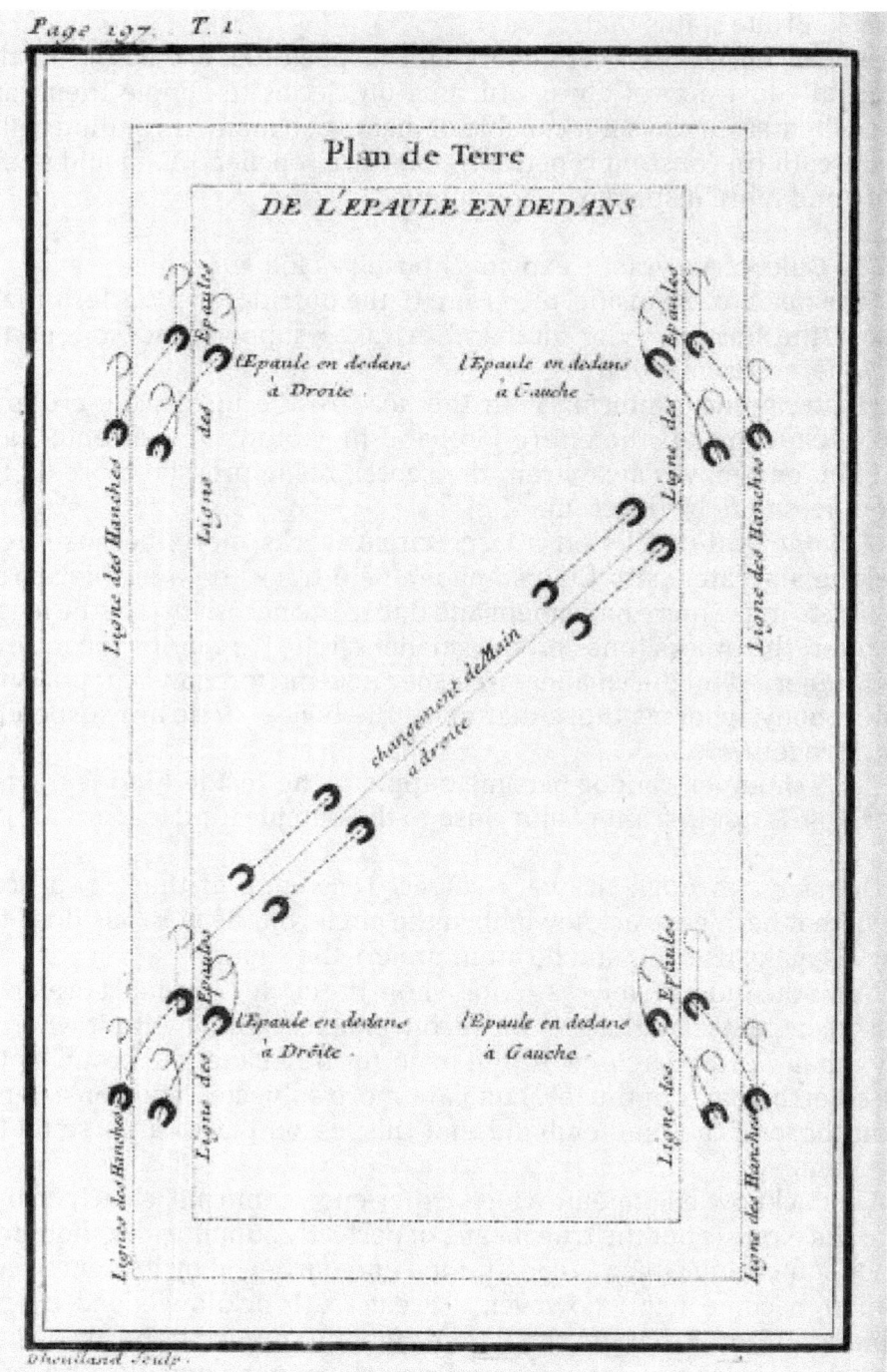

Legend
Plan de Terre de l'Épaule en Dedans - Diagram of the Shoulder-In
Ligne des Hanches - Track of the Haunches
Ligne des Épaules - Track of the Shoulders
L'Épaule en Dedans à Droite (Gauche) - Shoulder-in to the Right (Left)
Changement de Main à Droite - Change of Hand to the Right

and to carrying the head to the inside, it is then necessary to take him at a slow and slightly collected walk along the wall and place him so that his haunches follow one line and his shoulders follow another. The line of the haunches must be near the wall and the line of the shoulders must be about a foot and a half to two feet away from the wall, while keeping the horse bent in the direction in which he is moving. In other words, to explain myself more simply, instead of keeping a horse completely straight in the shoulders and the haunches on the straight line along the wall, it is necessary to turn his head and shoulders slightly inward, toward the center of the school, as if one actually wanted to turn him, and when he has assumed this oblique [angle] and circular [bend] posture [position], one must make him move forward along the wall while aiding him with the inside rein[9] and inside leg; he absolutely cannot go forward in this posture without stepping-over—or "*chevaler*[10]"—the inside front leg over the outside front and, similarly, the inside hind leg over the outside hind. This is easily seen in the figure of the shoulder-in which is at the beginning of this chapter and in the diagram of the same lesson[11], which will make this still more visible.

---

9   The aiding with the inside rein that is referred to here is the 'appui' or supportive rein contact in which the surface area of the rein is gently pressed against the inside neck muscle. The 'contact' with the inside curb bit, must not over-power the soft contact of the inside rein on the side of the horse's neck, if it does, the horse will only feel the sharp contact in the inside corner of his mouth and not the subtle coordiated aiding of inside leg in combination with inside supportive rein. — Editor's note.
10   The term "*chevaler*," as defined in Chapter IV, 'The Terms of the Art,' refers to "the movement of the horse as he leaves the side wall on two tracks, when his outside legs cross those on the inside." — Translator's note.
11   Regarding de la Guérinière's diagram of the shoulder-in which indicates that the horse should be moving on four tracks, the reader would benefit from the following excerpt taken from *The Complete Training Of Horse And Rider* by Alois Podhajsky:
"Nowadays there are different opinions as to the degree of the angle which the horse forms to the wall in the shoulder-in. In opposition to de la Guérinière's theory, it is maintained that the forehand should be taken in to such a degree that the inside hind leg follows exactly in the track of the outside foreleg, thus making a single track, so that three instead of four hoof prints appear. This interpretation generally leads to a sort of outline of a shoulder-in, and the inside foreleg does not cross sufficiently over the outside one. In this case, the purpose of the exercise—the bending of the three joints of the hind legs, the freer movements of the shoulders, the improvement of the contact with the bit, and the increase of suppleness and obedience—will not be achieved.
"Neither can the bending of the three joints of the hind legs—the chief object of this exercise—be achieved by the horse adopting an exaggerated position, because then the horse, instead of bringing the shoulder-in, will allow the hindquarters to fall out and exercise a kind of yielding to the leg; and yielding to

This lesson produces so many good results at once that I regard it as the first and the last of all those [lessons] that one can give to the horse to give him a complete suppleness and a perfect freedom in all parts of his body. This is so true that a horse which has been suppled following this principle, and then spoiled, either at the school or by some unskilled person, will become—if a true horseman puts him back in this lesson for a couple of days—as supple and comfortable as he was before.

Firstly, this lesson supples the shoulders, because the inside front leg, with each step that the horse takes in this posture, is stepping-over and *"chevalant"* in front of and above the outside leg, and the inside hoof is being placed above the outside hoof and in line with it; thus the movement which the shoulder is obliged to make in this action inevitably has a strengthenin effect on this part [the muscles of the shoulder and for lifting the front leg], which is easy to understand.

2. The shoulder-in prepares a horse for placing his weight on his haunches because, with each step that he takes in this posture, he brings the inside hind leg forward under the belly and places it over the outside hind leg, which he cannot do without bending the joints in his [inside] haunch. The horse is thus always on one haunch in one direction and on the other haunch in the other direction, and he consequently learns to bend his hocks underneath himself; this is what is called being on the haunches.

3. This same lesson prepares a horse for moving away from the spur [and leg] because being obliged to step over and pass one leg over the other, the front as much as the hind, with each movement, he acquires through this the ease to *"chevaler"* well the fore-arms and legs in both directions, which he must do in order to move sideways with ease. Such that, when one puts a horse in shoulder-in right, one prepares him for two-tracking [half-pass] to the left, because it is the right shoulder which is suppled in this posture; and when one puts him in the shoulder-in to the left, it is the left shoulder which is suppled and which prepares him to pass the left leg well in order to easily two-track to the right.

In order to change direction during the shoulder-in lesson (for example, from right to left), maintain the bend in the head and neck

---

the leg will never lead to a correct bending of the hind legs.

"When judging the shoulder-in, the expert should never allow himself to be involved in controversy as to which of the two doctrines is the correct one, but he should look to see whether the exercise is executed in the same manner on both reins. If, however, the horse has little position on one rein and as much as de la Guérinière demands on the other, then neither of the two versions is adhered to, but the exercise is presented just as the horse thinks fit, which is wrong and useless. A horse will always take his shoulder-in better on the rein of the side on which he accepts the bit and try to avoid the discomfort of the exercise by over-bending his neck on the other, the hollow, side."

and, upon leaving the wall, make the horse move with his shoulders and haunches straight on an oblique line until he has reached, in this posture, the line of the other wall; there, one must place his head to the left and the forehand to the inside and away from the line of the wall, while expanding [the previously shorter, side-the right side of the horse)] and making him cross the inside legs in this direction over the outside ones along the wall, and in the same manner that we have just explained for the right.

Since the horse will miss in the first lessons of the shoulder-in, whether by placing the croup too much to the inside or, on the other hand, by turning the shoulders too far to the inside and by leaving the line of the wall to avoid the constraint of passing and crossing his legs in a posture resulting in continuous contraction of the muscles which troubles him when he is not accustomed to it, the circle must therefore serve as the remedy for these defenses.

One will thus take him at a collected walk on a large circle and will, from time to time, take him away from the cross-stepping of the inside legs over those of the outside; such that, while enlarging the circle more and more, one will gradually arrive at the line of the wall and the horse will find himself in the posture of the shoulder-in, and, in this posture, one will make him take a few steps forward along the wall. One will then stop him, bend his head and neck, while playing with the bit in the mouth with the inside rein, praise him, and dismount.

If it happens that a horse holds back and resists out of malice and definitely is not willing to give in to the subjection of this lesson, it is necessary to leave it for awhile and return to the first principle of the lengthened and vigorous trot as much on a straight line as on a circle; and, when the horse has obeyed, one will return to the shoulder-in at the walk along the wall and, if he goes well for a few steps, one should halt, praise him, and dismount.

When the horse has started to obey the lesson of shoulder-in in both directions, one will teach him to work the corners well, which is the most difficult part of this lesson. For this, one must, in each corner —so to speak—at the end of each straight line, make the shoulders enter the corner while keeping the head placed to the inside; and, at the same time that one turns the shoulders onto the other [new direction] line, one must make the haunches, in their turn, pass in the same place on the corner as the shoulders did. It is with the inside rein and leg that the horse is carried forward in the corners. However, when one turns on to the other line [exiting the corner], this must be done with the outside rein by carrying the hand to the inside[12] and taking the moment when he has the inside [front] leg in the air and ready to return to the ground,

---

12 The author is referring to the convention, at the time of riding with the reins in one hand. When the word 'hand' is used it refers to the single hand holding the reins.

so that, by turning the hand at this time, the outside shoulder can pass over the inside; and, since the aid for turning is a type of half-halt, it is necessary, while turning the hand, to send the horse forward a little with both the calves. If the horse refuses to go into the corners with his croup by holding off in the hind end, and by clinging to the rider's inside leg (this is horses' most common resistance), it is necessary to use the inside heel [or spur, *talon*] while turning the shoulders onto the other line.

This is what I call *Passing through the corners*[13], which is not what is practiced by the majority of riders who are content to make the head and shoulders enter the corner and neglect to pass the croup there [through the same place theat the shoulders traveled]; so that the horse turns all in one piece instead of passing the haunches into the corner along the path the shoulders. [If ridden correctly] this passage of the shoulders and the haunches through the corners supples not only these two parts of the horse, but also the sides [of his body] as well, and it is this suppling of the sides which greatly augments the agility of the rest of the body.

If one examines the structure and the mechanics of the horse, one will be easily convinced of the usefulness of the shoulder-in, and one will acknowledge that my reasoning in support of this principle is taken from Nature itself, which is never self-contradictory providing it is not constrained beyond its limits. And, at the same time, if one pays attention to the movement of the horse's legs when the horse is on a circle with the head to the inside and the croup to the outside, it will be easy to understand that the haunches acquire the suppleness which one claims to give to the shoulders by means of the circle, since it is certain that the part which makes a greater movement is the one that becomes the most supple. Thus, I acknowledge the circle for giving horses the initial suppleness and also for punishing and correcting those who resist due to malice by putting the croup to the inside, in spite of the rider; however, I then view the shoulder-in as an indispensable lesson in order to achieve suppleness in the shoulders and to give them the facility to freely pass one leg over another, which is a perfection which must be present in all horses which are described as well-dressed[14] and well-trained[15].

---

13 *Prendre les coins*
14 *bien mis*
15 *bien dressé*

CHAPTER XII

On The Croup to The Wall (Haunches-Out)

Those who place a horse's head toward the wall to teach him to move sideways fall into an error which can be easily seen. This method makes the horse move by routine rather than from the hand and the legs; and when the wall is not available (as an object which fixes his view), he will not perfectly obey the hands and the legs, which are the only guides that must be used to direct a horse in all his gaits. Another problem which arises from this lesson is that, instead of passing the outside leg over the inside, he often passes it underneath for fear of catching himself with the iron of the leg that is on the ground or of striking his knee against the wall, as he raises the leg and carries it forward to pass it over the other.

De la Broue is of the same opinion when he advises only using the wall (in making horses two-track) for those that lean or pull on the hand; and, since it is better to place the head well away, rather than so close to the wall, he says that it is necessary to keep the horse two steps short of the wall, which means that the horse's head will be about five feet away from the wall.

Thus, I do not see why so many riders, in order to make the heels known to the horse, place his head to the wall while forcing him to move sideways with the leg, the spur, and even the long whip (which they have held by someone on foot). It is more reasonable, in my opinion, in order to avoid this embarrassment and the problems that could arise, to place his croup to the wall. This lesson is taken from the shoulder-in.

We have said in the preceding chapter that, in putting a horse in the shoulder-in to the right, one supples his right shoulder which gives fluency to the same right leg in crossing over the left legs when he moves sideways when traveling in the left direction [left half-pass]. The same is true of working him on the shoulder-in to the left, it is the shoulder on this side [left] which is suppled and which gives the same [left] leg the movement which it must have to freely cross over the right when asks the horse to move sideways on the right hand side [right half-pass].[16] Following this principle, which is indisputable, it is easy to convert the shoulder-in into the croup to the wall. One works from it in this manner.

When a horse is obedient in both directions in the shoulder-in lesson and when he consequently can freely pass the inside legs over the

---

16 Here the author is advocating the use of the shoulder-in left as suppling that will prepare the horse for half-pass right, (and vice versa).-Editor's note.

The croup to the wall

outside, it is necessary, while working him, to the right for example, after having turned him at the corner at one of tips of the *manège*, to stop him there with the croup toward the wall (the croup should be about two feet away from the wall so that he will not rub his tail against it) and instead of continuing to move forward [on the track to the right], one resists the horse with the hand and presses him with the left leg in order to remove him for awhile from the track to the right, and, if he obeys for two or three steps, one must stop him and praise him to make him know that this is what one is demanding of him.[17]

Since the newness of this lesson troubles a horse during the first days that one practices it, it is necessary, in the beginning, to guide him with the reins held separately [in two hands] and gently in order to better resist the shoulders; also it is necessary to not bend him at all, but to only give him a simple decision to move sideways without performing to perfection. As soon as the horse moves away from the leg for two or three steps without hesitation, one should stop him for a short while, praise him, and then resume moving sideways (while continuing to praise him for any obedience) until he has finally attained this posture at the end of the line, all along the wall, and at the other corner of the *manège*. After having let him rest for awhile in the place where he has finished, one then returns to the left on the same line while using the right leg to make him move sideways. One must give the same attention to praising him as soon as he has willingly obeyed for three or four steps and thus continue until he has arrived at the corner where one first began.

If the horse absolutely refuses to two-track in one of the two directions, this is proof that he has not been sufficiently suppled in the other direction. Thus it is necessary to put him in the shoulder-in [in the opposite direction]; in other words, if the horse refuses, for example, to move away from the left heel with the croup to the wall, which is the aid one gives for two-tracking to the right, it is necessary to return the horse to the shoulder-in to the left until he easily passes the left leg over the right. And when he finally finds himself, without noticing it, moving sideways with the croup to the wall to the right (which is the direction where we are supposing that he is disobedient), one turns his head and shoulders more and more to the inside until they are opposite the croup; thus by placing his head to the right and by continuing to

---

17 The author is describing tracking right down the long wall in shoulder-in right, after turning the corner, bring the shoulders around to the right and retrace the same track that was used for the shoulder-in, with the haunches-out to the wall, with mild right bending here the horse is moving off the left leg. The second part of this exercise is called 'croup to the wall to the right' even though the horse is slightly bent to the right (if allowed to bend at all) and the horse is tracking left (counter-clockwise around the manege). The name of the exercise is named for the bend or positioning, and not for the direction of travel. This is shown on the left side of the diagram on the facing page.—Editor's note.

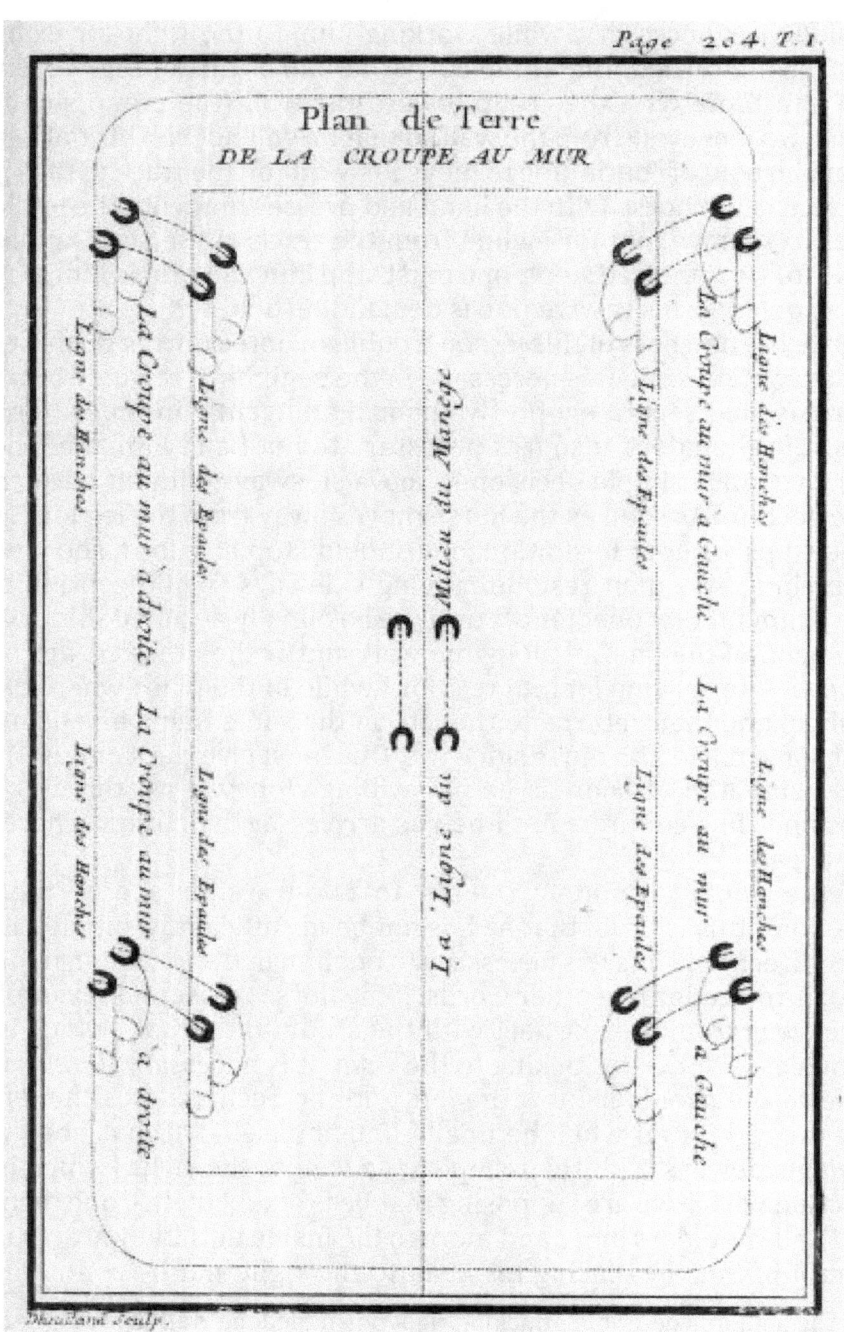

Legend
Plan de Terre de la Croupe au Mur — Diagram of the croup to the wall.
La Croupe au Mur à Droit — The croup to the wall to the right.
La Croupe au Mur à Gauche — The croup to the wall to the left.
Ligne des Épaules — line of the shoulders.
Ligne des Hanches — Line of the haunches.
La Ligne du Milieu du Manège — The centerline of the manège (school).

make him move away from the left leg, as if he were still moving in the shoulder-in to the left, he will find himself moving sideways to the right. Similarly, if the horse refuses to move away from the right heel, which is to two-track to the left, it is necessary to put him in a shoulder-in to the right and gradually, by turning the shoulders well in until they are opposite the croup, the horse will be moving away from the right heel and consequently two-tracking to the left.

Following what we have just explained, it is easy to observe that what we call the shoulder-in in one direction (on one hand) becomes the shoulder-out when one places the croup towards the wall, because the same shoulder continues its movement even though the horse goes in the other direction (on the other hand). However, since in the posture of the croup to the wall, the horse (while moving sideways) must be almost straight in the shoulders and the haunches, the action of the shoulder is thus more circular and, consequently, the movement is more stressful and difficult for a horse than that of the shoulder-in. Given some attention, this difference will be easily understood and, at the same time, it will prove that one of the advantages of the shoulder-in is to teach a horse to pass and *"chevaler"* each leg freely over the other and that this is a remedy for all the mistakes he could make when one is teaching him to two-track.

Once a horse begins to obey in freely moving sideways in both directions with the croup to the wall, it is necessary to place him in the posture necessary to two-track gracefully, which is done by observing three essential things.

The first is to make the shoulders move in front of the haunches; otherwise, the circular movement of the outside leg and shoulder, which makes the grace and suppleness of this part evident, will no longer be present. It is necessary that at least half the shoulders move in front of the croup, so that (supposing, for example, one were moving to the right) the position of the right hind foot will be on the line of the front leg (as can be seen in the diagram). Because, if the croup moves in front of the shoulders, the horse is stiffened and the inside hind leg, which is moving and being placed more forward than the inside front leg, makes the horse more enlarged in the hind-end than the forehand and, consequently, on the hocks, because, in order to have the weight on the haunches, a horse must contract the hind-end while moving.

Secondly, attention must be given when a horse begins to move sideways freely with the croup to the wall, to bend him in the direction in which he is moving. A nice bend makes a horse graceful, draws his outside shoulder in and gives it a free and forward action. In order to make the horse accustomed to bending himself in the direction he is going, it is necessary, at the end of each line of the croup to the wall, after having stopped him, to draw his head with the inside rein while playing with the bit in the mouth; and when he yields to this movement, he must be praised with the hand on the side to which he has been bent. One must observe the same thing while finishing on the other hand and heel; in this way the horse will gradually develop the habit of moving bent and of looking where he is going while moving sideways.

The third thing that one must still observe in this lesson is to have the horse describe the two lines, which are that of the shoulders and that of the haunches, without moving forward or back so that they are parallel. Since that comes in part from the horse's nature, it usually happens that those which are heavy or pull on the hand leave the line by moving forward too much; this is why it is necessary to resist these with the bridle hand without aid from the legs. On the other hand, it is necessary to chase forward those who have the bad habit of resisting the bracing of their back by using the inner thighs, the calves, and sometimes even the spurs, according to how much they are holding back. With this precaution, one will maintain both types in obedience to and control by the hand and the legs.

In order to avoid the situation in which a horse, while moving sideways, falls into the fault of crossing over and of pushing or throwing himself on one heel or the other, despite the aid of the rider, it is necessary (at the end of each short lesson) to direct the horse between the heels straight on one track on the centerline; one thus also teaches him, on the same line, to rein-back straight in the balance of the heels.

Even though the shoulder-in lesson and that of the croup to the wall, which must be inseparable, are excellent for giving a horse the suppleness, the nice bend and posture in which a horse must move in order to handle himself with grace and lightness, it is not necessary *to* abandon the trotting lesson on the straight line and on the circles; these are the first principles to which one must always return in order to maintain and confirm the horse in a bold action which is supported by the shoulders and the haunches. In this way, one diverts a horse and relieves him from the constraint that is demanded by the posture of the shoulder-in and the croup to the wall. This is the order which must be observed in order to make these lessons profitable.

Of the three short lessons that one will do each day and each time that one rides a horse which will be advanced enough to execute what we have stated in this chapter, the first must be the shoulder-in done at the walk; and, after two changes of direction, which must be done on one track (because it is not at all necessary to still move sideways), one places the croup to the wall in both directions and one finishes it on a straight and single track at the walk on the centerline of the *manège*. The second short lesson must be done at a brisk trot which is sustained and on one track; and one finishes in the same action on the centerline of the place without placing the horse's croup to the wall. For the third and last short lesson, it is necessary to return to the shoulder-in at the walk, then the croup to the wall, and always to finish it by going straight on the centerline. While thus combining these three lessons of the shoulder-in, the trot, and the croup to the wall, one will gradually see a horse's suppleness and obedience develop and increase; and, as we have stated, suppleness and obedience are the first two qualities which a horse must have in order to be trained.

CHAPTER XIII

On The Usefulness of The Pillars

The pillars are the invention of de Pluvinel who had the honor of teaching Louis XIII to ride. He left us a Traité de Cavalerie whose plates are viewed as a curiosity in regard to the engraving and the dress of this prince's noblemen.

The Duke of Newcastle is not at all in favor of the pillars. He states "that one disables a horse in the pillars and wrongly agitates a horse in order to make him raise the forehand, thereby hoping to place him on the haunches; that this method is against nature and discourages all horses; that the pillars place a horse on the hocks because, even though he bends the hocks, he does not move the haunches forward under himself to keep his balance and is supporting his forehand on the cavesson ropes."

What has caused this famous author to rebel so strongly against the use of the pillars is that, in his time, most of the masters were making use of this method to initially raise a horse's forehand before he was steady in the piaffe. In this way, they were, without a doubt, placing a horse on the hocks and were teaching him to rear rather than to raise the forehand willingly. However, if, in the beginning, instead of intending to make the horse come off the ground, one uses the pillars to teach him to passage in one place without moving forward, back, or to the side, which is the action of the piaffe, one will see that this cadence, which is easier to produce in the pillars than when free, places the horse in a nice posture, gives him a noble and elevated gait, gives the shoulders a bold and free movement, and the haunches a smooth and supple elasticity. All of these qualities are sought after for a parade horse and to form a nice passage. However, since much skill, patience, and time are necessary to regulate a horse in this strong and elevated air of the passage, which is given by the pillars when used intelligently, it is not surprising that they cause so many problems for those who use them with any intent other than to first succeed at the piaffe.

The piaffe

A knowledgeable master said, with reason, that the pillars give spirit to horses because the fear of punishment keeps those who are bored and lazy in a brilliant action; but the pillars still have the advantage of calming those that are naturally hot and angry, because the action of the piaffe, which is a regular, sustained, and elevated movement, makes them pay attention to what they are doing. This is why I regard the pillars as a means, not only to recover the resourcefulness, vigor, gracefulness, lightness, and disposition of a horse, but also as a means to giving these greatest qualities to those that are lacking in them.

In the beginning, attention must first be given (when putting a horse in the pillars) to attach the cavesson ropes so that they are short and of equal length in order that the horse's shoulders are level with the pillars and only the head and neck are above them; in this way, the horse will not be able to pass the croup under the cavesson ropes, as sometimes happens. One must then move behind the croup with the long whip and remain far enough away so there is no chance of being kicked; one then puts the horse to the right and to the left by using the long whip on the ground and sometimes lightly on the rump. This manner of putting a horse to one side and the other teaches him to cross the legs, coordinates him in his movement, and gives him the fear of punishment. When he has obeyed this aid, it is necessary to chase him forward and, as soon as he brings himself into the ropes, to stop him and praise him in order to let him know that this is what one is demanding of him. It is not at all necessary to demand anything else of him until he has been confirmed in the obedience of putting himself to the right and to the left and moving forward from the long whip following the rider's will.

There are some horses of a spirited and malicious nature who, before putting themselves to the side from the long whip and moving forward into the ropes, use all the defenses that their malice makes available to them. Some, who are very anxious, stamp instead of piaffing, others rear and bound in the ropes, and still others increase their frequent kicking and back up or throw themselves against the pillars. However, since most of these problems come more often from the impatience of the person who punishes them improperly in the beginning, rather than from the horse's nature, it is easy to remedy this by simply being satisfied (as we have just stated) in making him move sideways and forward from the whip, which is the only obedience that one must demand from a horse the first time that one places him in the pillars.

Attention must also be given to making the horses who have a sluggish croup and no movement in the haunches kick in the pillars. This action loosens their hocks and makes them use their haunches, gives the croup some play, and places all the strength of this part in motion. Everyone is not of this opinion, and most say that one must never teach a horse to kick.

However, experience makes it evident that a horse which has never been made to kick has stiff haunches and drags them when working. Moreover, it is definitely easy to rid the horse of this fault, which would be necessary if one were to make him accustomed to kicking out of malice; but once one has found the haunches to be loose enough, one must prevent him from kicking by punishing him with the switch in front at the moment that he gives this action and one has not asked for it.

When the horse stops moving to the side and when he brings himself forward and straight into the ropes, it is thus necessary to animate him with the tongue and the long whip in order to get from him some cadence of the trot in place, straight and in the middle of the ropes, which is what one calls the piaffe; and, as soon as this is achieved, one must praise him and unhook him in order not to discourage him. If he continues to obey in this lesson for a few days, it is necessary to lengthen the cavesson ropes until the pillars are opposite the horse's body, so that he will have the freedom to bring himself into the ropes better and so that he can raise his legs with more grace and ease. Even though he continues to do well, one must not, as a result, have long sessions until he has become accustomed to obeying without getting angry; and, thus, it is necessary to make the lessons as long as his disposition, his strengths, and his wind will permit; and this without the help of the long whip with the rider keeping himself only behind the croup.

In order to accustom the horse to doing the piaffe without aid from the voice or the long whip, one allows him to finish the cadence himself, while remaining behind him without making any movement or any sound with the tongue until he has stopped completely; and just when he has stopped, one must use the long whip briskly on the croup and the rump. This punishment puts the whole nature in motion and keeps the horse fearful so that, when he has become accustomed to this lesson, one will be able to remain behind him for as long as one judges proper, without aiding him, and he will continue to piaffe. When one wants to stop him, one alerts him with the voice by familiarizing him with the term *Hola* (Whoa), and one moves from behind the croup; the horse should them be praised and returned to the stable. However, this lesson should only be practiced when a horse has started to properly understand what one is demanding of him and when he no longer moves to the side or resists.

Once a horse has been confirmed in this air of the piaffe which is produced between the pillars, it is thus necessary (and not any earlier) to begin having the horse come off the ground by sometimes making him raise himself in *pesades*[18] and *courbettes*, by lightly touching him

---

18   In regard to de la Guérinière's reference to the pesade in this chapter (formal definition of the pesade is given in Chapter V, *The Gaits of the Horse*—-ARTICLE III, "The Artificial Gaits," the reader should take note of the differentiation between the pesade and the levade made by Podhajsky in

with the switch in front and by animating him with the long whip behind. Not only is the *courbette* a pretty air, but it makes the horse more elevated in his forehand, and it has an action in the shoulder which is more sustained than at the piaffe which prevents the horse from stamping (*"trepigner"*), an unpleasant action where the horse hits the dirt in a rapid tempo; instead the piaffe is a sustained and elevated action of the shoulder with the forearm high in the air and bent at the knee, which gives much grace to a horse. In order to prevent a horse from raising himself against the rider's will (which will produce disorganized leaps without regularity or obedience), it is necessary to begin and end each short lesson with the piaffe, so that the horse raises himself when one wants and piaffes as well. One will thus avoid a habit which is the fault of the improperly-run schools.

Since it is dangerous to ride a horse in the pillars when he has not become accustomed to them, one must not endanger a rider between the pillars before the horse has been trained and is obedient to the degree demanded according to the principles that we have just described. Likewise, when one begins to ride him in the pillars, one continues with the same methods that were used before the rider was on the horse; in other words, one must put him to the right and to the left while aiding him with the legs in order to make him bring himself forward into the ropes. He will gradually becomes accustomed to piaffing from the hand and the legs, as he previously did from the long whip.

Amateurs from the Spanish cavalry held the piaffe in high regard and greatly valued horses who moved with this air and whom they called *Piaffadores.* However, they gave their horses an uncomfortable and irregular gait because they did not supple their shoulders at all and did not make the heels known to the horses. This is why they only worked the forearm, did not have any sort of firm and light contact with the mouth, did not have the horse at all in the balance of the heels, and, consequently, not in perfect obedience to the hand and the legs, which is the perfection of the air of the piaffe.

The Complete Training Of Horse And Rider: "Up to the nineteenth century the riding masters knew only the pesade in which the horse lifts his forehand off the ground with lowered hocks, his body forming an angle of forty-five degrees to the ground. Beginning with the twentieth century an exercise was introduced in which the height of the body from the ground was reduced and the body held at an angle of thirty degrees to the ground. This was called the levade and used as a model for many equestrian monuments. If the horse lifts himself higher from the ground at an angle of more than forty-five degrees and does not bend his hind legs, he does not perform any classical movement but simply rears up."— *Translator's Note.*

CHAPTER XIV

On The Passage

After having given a horse the initial suppleness by means of the trot on a single track, on the straight line and on circles, and after having made him round, taught him to pass his legs in the circular posture of the shoulder-in, made him obedient to the heels in the croup to the wall and collected in the piaffe in the pillars (all these lessons contributing to the development of suppleness and obedience which are, as we have stated, the first qualities which a horse must have in order to be trained), one must next work to adjust the horse or, in other words, to regulate him and to make him work properly in the air, as well as his disposition will permit. The passage is the first gait that deals with precision. We have already defined it in the chapter on the artificial gaits and we have stated that it is a trot or a step which is collected, measured, and cadenced and that, in this movement, the horse must sustain the legs that are in the air (one front, the other behind) which are diagonally opposite as in the trot but which are more collected and sustained than at the ordinary trot. We have also stated that the horse, with each step that he takes, must not advance or place the leg that is in the air more than a foot beyond the one that is on the ground. This gait, which makes a horse patient and improves his memory, is very noble and often makes an officer visible on an inspection or parade day. The horse's action in the passage is the same as in the piaffe: therefore, in order to have an accurate conception of both, it is necessary to view the piaffe as a passage in one place without moving forward or back, and the passage is, so to speak, a piaffe in which the horse moves forward about a foot with each movement. In the piaffe, the knee of the front leg that is in the air must be level with the elbow of that leg, and this leg must be bent so that the toe is raised as high as the middle of the knee of the leg that is on the ground. The back leg must not be raised as high, since then the horse would not be on the haunches; the toe of the leg that is in the air should only be as high as the middle of the cannon bone of the leg that is on the ground. As for the passage, since the movement is more forward than that of the piaffe, the front leg must not be raised as high; the toe of the foot that is in the air should only be as high as the cannon bone of the leg that is on the ground, and the back leg should be slightly higher than the fetlock of the other leg.

There are several things to observe in the passage: namely, the posture the horse must be in when he passages (be it on a single track or on two tracks), the cadence or measure in which he must passage, and the aids the rider uses to adjust him in the air.

The Passage

The most skilled riding masters agree that one of the most important things for putting a horse in a nice posture is the nice bend one gives him while working; however, this nice bend is explained differently by the skilled masters of the art. Some want a horse to simply bend in an arc which is no more than a half-bend where only one of the horse's eyes is looking into the circle. Others want the horse to make the half-circle; in other words, they want both his eyes to be looking inside the line. One must agree that, in both bends, the horse is graceful, but I believe that the bend in an arc (which is only a half-bend) does not constrain a horse as much and keeps him more elevated in front than when he is more bent; and in the latter posture, most horses are arched or, in other words, lower the nose too much and curve the head and neck downward.

Those that acknowledge the half-bend keep their horses straight in the shoulders and the haunches, or only keep half of the haunch to the inside; those that want a greater bend keep the haunches as much to the inside as the head, which makes a half-circle from the head to the tail, and this is called *"les deux bouts dedans"* (the two ends to the inside). This posture makes a horse appear more on the haunches, because he is more contracted behind.

One can acknowledge these different postures by applying them differently in accord with the different structure of each horse. There are few horses which are well proportioned throughout their entire body; some are too short in the loins, and others are too long in the body.

Those that are well proportioned, which is to say neither too short nor too long in the loins, must be kept with half the haunch to the inside so that, instead of the haunches being completely straight on the line of the shoulders, the outside hind leg must be placed on the track of the inside leg (which means that half of the haunches are to the inside). This is what is properly called the half-haunch to the inside. This posture is very nice and agrees very well with horses who have good conformation and who carry themselves well.

Horses who are short in the loins must be kept straight in the shoulders and the haunches, with only a half-bend, which makes them look to the inside with only one eye. If one were to place them in a more collected posture, by bending them too much and keeping their haunches to the inside, they would be too constrained and would not have a nice movement of the shoulder, because most horses with this build usually resist. Consequently it is necessary to give them a passage which is freer and more forward than that given to horses which are naturally equally balanced.

In the passage with *"les deux bouts dedans"* (the two ends to the inside), the head is placed well to the inside, with the haunches placed as much to the inside as the head, so that the horse is rounded throughout his entire body and forms a half-circle. This posture was invented in order to shorten and give the appearance of being on the haunches to those horses who are too long in the body, as well as the head and neck, and who are not graceful enough and would not be able to collect themselves as well if one were to put them completely on one track. This posture is no more than the croup to the wall in reverse; in other words, instead of making a horse move to the side in the croup to the wall with the shoulders to the inside of the school, in *"les deux bouts dedans"* (the two ends to the inside), one places the shoulders opposite the wall and the croup near the center, so that the horse is almost on two tracks.

After having examined which of these three postures best suits the horse, in accord with his nature and his build, one must next regulate the cadence of his air. The cadence of a horse's passage must be understood as being the movement of the collected trot, which is sustained in the forehand and continues in an equal beat without either resistance or hurrying. This movement, which is as difficult to develop in a horse as collecting him while walking, depends upon the coordination of the rider's aids and also upon a horse's suppleness and obedience. That is why it is not at all necessary to passage a horse with the precision that is so greatly desired between the pillars. This practice serves as the model of the nice passage and even though a horse is advanced enough so that one can demand accurate lessons from him, one must never abandon the first lessons which cannot be overly emphasized. Thus, each time one rides a horse (no matter how advanced he may be), it is necessary, of the three short lessons, to at least demand a shoulder-in followed by the croup to the wall and, depending upon the situation, to even put him back in the trot.

In order to collect a horse in this beautiful movement of the passage, which produces the free, sustained, and equally forward movement of the shoulder, attention must be given to his nature and to his strengths. For example, the horses that resist consequently hold back the action of the shoulder. They must be less constrained, and when they overly resist (due to malice or another reason), they must even be vigorously chased forward with both legs and sometimes even the spurs, thus abandoning for awhile the regulated accuracy of the passage in order to maintain them in fear of and obedience to the rider's punishment (which they must have). On the other hand, those that, due to a natural timidity, throw themselves on the hand must be kept more collected and supported by the hand rather than regulated by the legs. With these precautions, both will be kept in their true air.

The change of direction in the passage must be done on two tracks on an oblique line with half the shoulders moving before the croup, so that the outside front leg is on the line of the inside hind leg; and, so that the horse remains in balance between the two heels, it is not necessary that he make a single beat with more fear of the rider's outside leg than the inside leg will permit. For this, it is necessary that the rider know how to properly use his hand and his legs.

In the passage on two tracks, the horse must make as many movements with the back feet as with the front. It often happens that the horse's back feet stop in one place, while the front feet steal some ground by taking two or three steps. This fault is called unfolding the shoulder. Another fault, which is still greater, occurs when the horse's front feet stop, but the back feet continue to move (which is referred to as bringing to a standstill or setting the back). Since the rider is looking at the position of the head and neck and the action of the shoulders, it is easier for him to adjust the movements of the horse's front feet than to keep the croup and the back feet in an equal degree of accuracy. It is nevertheless necessary to acquire ease in doing both in order to be able to promptly correct these problems; this depends upon the application of the hand and the sensitivity of the heel.

It is necessary to still remember that one of the most subtle aids is to make the horse's outside shoulder and forearm pass over the inside shoulder and forearm while passaging on two tracks. In order to grasp this moment well, states the knowledgeable de la Broue, it is necessary to feel which foot is on the ground and which foot is in the air; then to turn the bridle hand when the front leg on the side he is turning is in the air and ready to return to the ground, so that, while then raising the other front leg, he must move the outside shoulder and forearm forward by passing it over the inside shoulder and forearm. He adds that it requires great facility with the aids to grasp this moment well; because, if one turns the hand when the horse's inside leg is too high, instead of enlarging the outside shoulder and leg, it is the inside shoulder and leg which become enlarged; and if one turns the hand when he puts the inside foot on the ground, he does not have enough time to freely pass the outside shoulder and leg.

Before finishing this chapter, it is good to again notice that of the three postures we have just discussed (in which we can put the horse in the passage), there are two of them which can only be permitted in the confines of a small school or for the sport of racing; they are that of the half-haunch and that of *"les deux bouts dedans"* (the two ends to the inside). However, when the horse is held in a noble and elevated step, be it at the head of a troop on days of inspection or parade or on holidays, one must not ask him for this school movement at all but rather keep him straight in the shoulders and the haunches, with only a half-bend in the direction he is going, in order to make his forehand more graceful.

CHAPTER XV

Changes of Hand and The Way to Doubler

The line that a horse makes when he goes from the right to the left or the left to the right is what is usually called the change of hand, and, since this lesson is based in part on the method used to "*doubler*," we will first explain what it is to "*doubler*" a horse.

The *manège*, which is considered to be a place where horses are exercised, must be a long square, and the division of this square into several other larger or smaller forms is what is called the wide "*doubler*" and the narrow "*doubler.*"

This practice of the "*doubler*," be it wide or narrow (according to the rider's will), makes the horse attentive to the aids and prompt in obeying the hand and the legs; but the difficulty with this action is to turn the shoulders at the end of the line of the square without the croup becoming out of line. For this, it is necessary, while turning at the end of each line of the square, to form a quarter of a circle with the shoulders and to keep the haunches in the same place. In this action, the inside hind leg must remain in one place and the three other legs (the two front and the outside hind leg) must turn in a circular manner around the inside hind, which serves as a pivot. When the shoulders have reached the line of the haunches, one continues to pass straight between the heels to the other corner of the square. This lesson is repeated at the end of each line, except in the corners where the angles of the square are formed by the meeting of the two walls. The haunches must therefore follow in the path of the shoulders; in other words, through the angles of the corner and at the same time that the shoulders are turned onto the other line.

It is from the four corners of the square and in the middle of the *manège* that the proportions observed in the well-run schools are taken, and these serve to maintain the order which is necessary in the wide and narrow changes of hand, the voltes and the half-voltes; because, even though some horsemen neglect this regularity, it is not proper to copy them in a practice which is not accurate.

There are wide changes of hand and narrow changes of hand, counter changes of hand, and changes of hand in reverse.

The wide change of hand is the path the horse makes from one wall to another, be it on one or two tracks or on an oblique line.

The two lines of the wide change of hand on two tracks in the diagram will give an idea of the proportions which must be observed in order to do a wide change.

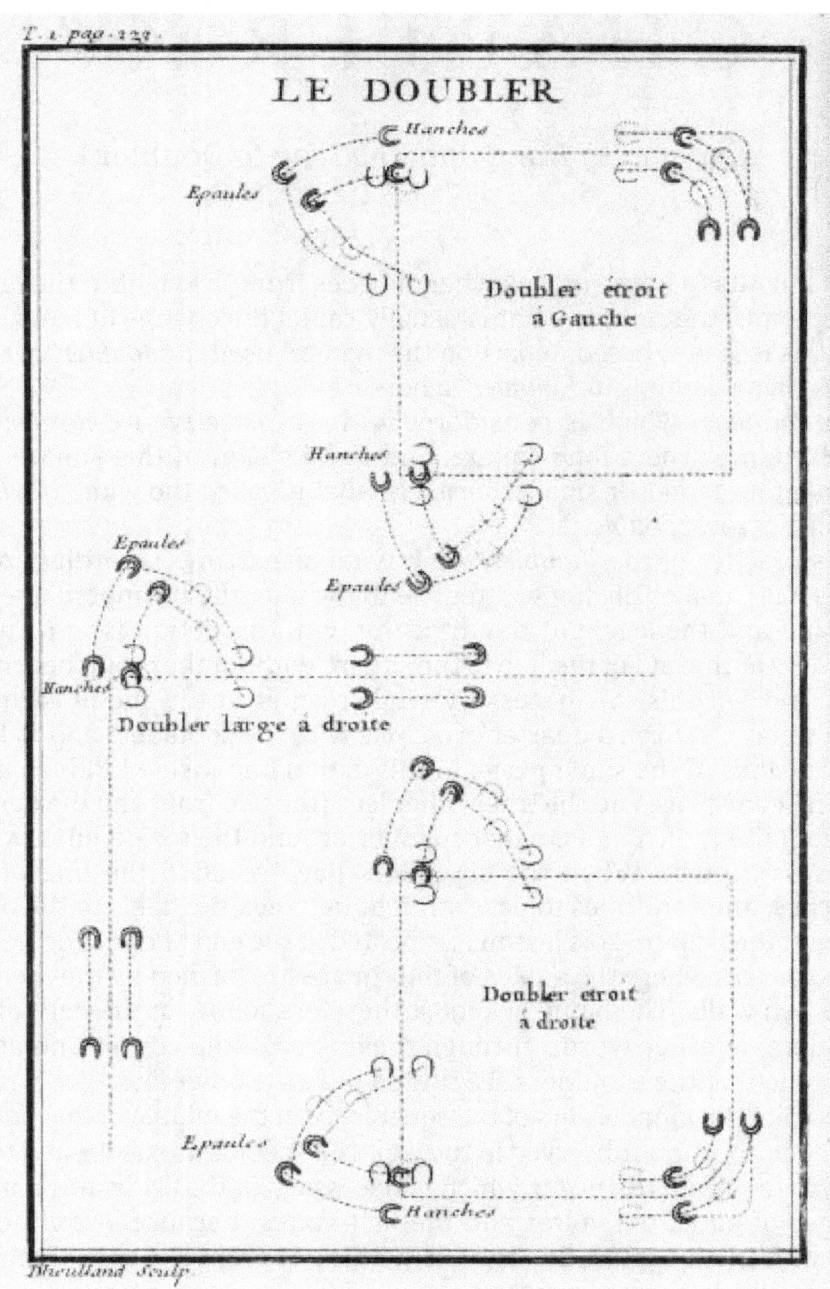

Legend
Le Doubler - The "Doubler"
Doubler Ètroit à Gauche - Narrow *Doubler* to the Left
Doubler Ètroit à Droite - Narrow *Doubler* to the Right
Doubler arge à Droite - Wide *Doubler* to the Right
Epaules ¯ Shoulders
Hanches - Haunches

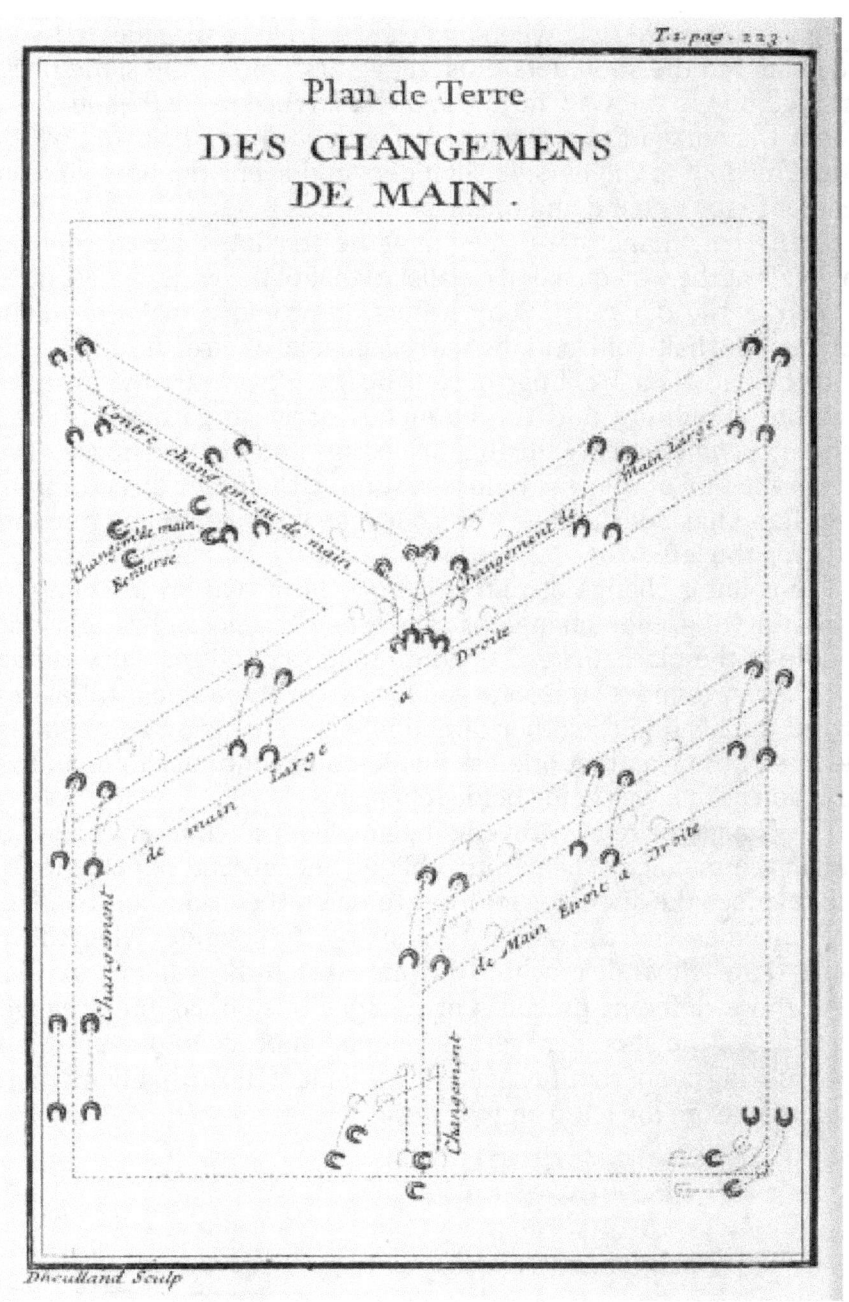

Legend
Plan de Terre des Changements de Main - Diagram of the Changes of Hand
Contre Changement de Main - Counter Change of Hand
Changement de Main Renversé - Change of Hand, Reversed
Changement de Main Large - Wide Change of Hand
Changement de Main Large à Droite - Wide Chage of Hand to the Right
Changement de Main Ètroit à Droite - Narrow Change of Hand to the Right

It must be noted that, when one changes rein to the side on two tracks, the head and the shoulders must move first and in the same posture as for the croup to the wall; however, the difference being that, in the change of rein, the horse must move forward with each step he takes, which gives much freedom to the outside shoulders and keeps the horse in continual obedience to the hand and the legs.

The narrow change of rein begins at the first line of the narrow "*doubler*" and ends at the wall on a line parallel to that of the wide change of rein (as is seen in the diagram). Some riders, improperly, make no distinction between the half-volte and the narrow change of direction.

At the end of each change of rein, be it wide or narrow, it is necessary that the shoulders and the haunches arrive together. This is called *Fermer le changement* (closing the change), so that the horse's four legs are on the line of the wall before resuming the other direction. Only the right hand has been shown here, because it is easy to imagine the same lines for the left.

The counter change of rein is composed of two lines. The first is the beginning of a wide change of rein; when the horse has arrived at the middle of the place, instead of continuing to go in the same direction, it is necessary to move straight ahead for two or three steps and, after having placed the head in the other direction, one returns on an oblique line to the line of the wall that one has just left and continues to go in the same direction as one was going before changing.

The change of rein in reverse begins like the counter change of rein, and, in the middle of the second oblique line, instead of going to the wall, one reverses the shoulder in order to be on the other hand. Refer to the diagram where one can see the reversing of the shoulder when the horse is going to the left while reaching the place he left the wall to go to the right.

All these different practices of changes of rein, counter changes, and reversing of the shoulder were developed in order to prevent the horses from moving out of routine, which is the fault of those that work more from habit than from the hand and the legs.

CHAPTER XVI

On The Canter

Since we have already given (in the chapter on the natural gaits) the definition of the different movements that a horse makes while cantering (be it on the right or the left, when he is on the wrong lead or disunited), we need only discuss here the characteristics of the canter, the way to feel it, and the rules which must be observed in order to canter a horse well.

The canter provides three definite advantages, which are to make the horse's mouth more sensitive, increase wind, and reduce the excess energy of a horse who has too much back.

All horsemen agree that the canter develops feel and makes the mouth sensitive because during the action made by the horse while cantering (both his shoulders and forearms being raised and, following this movement, the front legs returning to the ground together), the horse is naturally inclined to make contact with the bit; thus the rider has the time, at this moment, to make him feel the effect of the bridle.

The canter improves the wind, since the horse must stretch all the parts of his body in order to better distribute his strength, the chest muscles become dilated and the lungs expand with more air, which provides freer breathing.

The canter reduces the excess energy of certain horses who use their back for disunited leaps (which make a rider uncomfortable and out of balance), the explanation being that since in the movement made by a horse while cantering the front legs are not close to the back legs, the back (which is the strongest part of the body) must be lowered in this action; consequently, its strength is lessened.

This must be understood as being the extended canter, which is proper for these types of horses, because the collected canter will give them an opportunity to continue with their disobedience.

It is a practiced rule by all the skilled masters that a horse must not be cantered until he has been suppled at the trot, so that he brings himself forward at the canter without leaning or pulling on the hand. It is thus necessary to wait until his whole body is supple, until he is rounded in the inside shoulder, is obedient to the heels at the passage with the croup to the wall, and has become light at the piaffe in the pillars. As soon as he has reached this degree of obedience, despite the little that one unsettles him in the canter, he will do it willingly.

One must canter him in the posture of the shoulder-in, not only to make him free and obedient, but also to rid him of the bad habit (that

The galopade

almost all horses have) of cantering with the inside hind leg open and held apart from, and outside of, the line of the inside front leg. This fault is considerable enough to make a rider very uncomfortable and ill at ease. As is easy to notice in most horses that canter, for example on the right lead (which is the way to canter hunters and hack horses), one will see that they have almost the entire left shoulder brought back and that they are tipped to the left. The reason for this is natural; while cantering with the right hind held open and apart from the left, the bone of the horse's haunch, in this case, pushes and throws the rider to the outside and places him off balance. Thus to remedy this fault, it is necessary to canter the horse in the shoulder-in to teach him to bring the inside hind leg close to the outside leg, and to lower the haunches. Once he has become suppled and broken into this posture, it is easy for him to then canter with the haunches collected and on the line of the shoulders, so that the hind end chases the forehand, which is the true and nice canter.

Another fault that most riders have is that, in the beginning, they do not apply themselves at all to feeling their canter, which is nevertheless essential. It is for this reason that I have found it appropriate here to teach a means of feeling the canter in a short while. I have taken it from an old master who was held in high repute with the race horses.

This method is to take a hack horse who has a long and extended walk and to concentrate on feeling the position of the front feet. In order to feel this position, it is necessary, in the beginning, to look at the movement of the shoulder in order to see which foot is on the ground and which is in the air, while counting the movement in the head and saying: *one, two.* For example, when the left front foot is on the ground, one must say to oneself *one* and when the right front foot is, in its turn, on the ground, one must say *two* and so on, continuing to count *one, two.*

It is not very difficult to count by looking at this positioning of the feet. However, the main point is to transfer this feeling into the thighs and inner thighs so that the impression made, for example, by the left foot when it is put on the ground transfers into the left inner thigh, without the rider looking at the movement of the shoulder anymore, and while still counting (as was done while looking at it) *one* similarly, when the right foot is on the ground, it is necessary, without looking at the movement of the leg, to say *two.* With a small amount of attention given to observing this method, one will, in a short while, feel in his inner thighs which foot is on the ground and which foot is in the air. When one is very sure of this at the walk, one must practice the same thing at the trot, which is a more elevated and faster movement and consequently, more difficult to feel. This is why it is necessary, in this gait, to begin by looking at the movement of the shoulder, to be sure of its position and to transfer this feeling to the inner thighs, as was done at the walk.

Once one is able to feel the position of the front legs well at the trot, without looking at the shoulder, one will soon feel it at the canter, because the positioning of the front feet at the canter is done in two beats, as at the trot: one, two.

As one becomes confirmed in his canter, it will be easy to feel when the horse becomes disunited, because a disunited horse has a gait which is so uncomfortable that, even if one is not deep in the saddle, a person would have to be lacking in any feeling to not realize the disorder caused by this irregular change in the seat.

Even though to feel the canter well may seem to merit more attention than the science of it, it is nevertheless absolutely necessary to know in order to ride a horse within the rules. Any rider who does not feel the horse's canter can never pass as a horseman.

De la Broue states that the nice canter must be shortened in the forehand and be active in the haunches. This definition is for the school canter which we are speaking about here, because the hunt or hacking canter (which we will discuss in the chapter on Hunters) must be extended. This activity in the hindquarters, which forms the true cadence of the canter, is only achieved by the sending forward, the half-halts, and frequent yielding of the hand. The sending forward settles a horse faster than his ordinary cadence; the half-halt supports the horse's forehand after having settled him for a few steps; and the yielding of the hand is the reward which must immediately follow obedience by the horse and which avoids the bad habit of leaning on the bit.

Once the horse may be easily sent forward, is steady and obedient to the hand at the half-halt, and does not lose the head position at all in the yielding of the hand, one must then put him in a collected canter. This is where the hindend chases and accompanies the forehand in an even cadence without dragging the haunches, and where the sending forward and the half-halts are imperceptible, so to speak, and are only sensed by the horse.

In order to attain this cadenced and collected canter, one must carefully examine the nature of each horse, in order to properly provide the lessons which are suited to him.

Horses who resist must be extended and set on long straight lines before adjusting their canter, on the other hand, those that have too much energy must be kept in a slow, shortened canter which prevents their wanting to rush too much and which, at the same time, improves their wind.

It is not always necessary to canter horses that have too much back on straight lines, but rather on circles, since they are forced to keep themselves more collected for turning than for going straight. This action lessens the power of their back, keeps their attention, and removes their spirit and their desire to pull on the hand.

There are other horses who, with enough back, are weak or feel pain, be it in the shoulders, the legs, the fetlocks, or the feet, due to nature or to their own strength; they usually are ungraceful at the canter. One must demand long sessions from them in order to preserve their heart and spare their small amount of spirit.

There are still two other types of horses whose way of cantering is different. Some swim while cantering; in other words, they extend their front legs by raising them too high; on the other hand, others canter too close to the ground. In order to solve the problem of those that swim, it is necessary to lower the hand and push the heel down while leaning on the stirrups when the front legs are on the ground. For those that canter too close to the ground and lean on the bit, it is necessary to yield the hand when the forehand is in the air, while rousing them with the calves, and when their front feet are returning to the ground, to keep the hand close to oneself without leaning too much on the stirrups.

One must always canter a horse on one track until he easily canters in both directions because if one were to push him too early into moving sideways (in other words, before he has acquired the suppleness and the freedom of the canter) he would toughen in his mouth, become stiff in his forehand, and be given a reason to fight back. One will easily know when he is ready to canter with the haunches-in because in placing his croup to the wall (if he feels supple and free enough to obey) he will, however little one animates him with the tongue and activates him with the outside leg, take the canter on his own. One should continue for only a few steps, stopping and praising after. This lesson should be practiced from time to time until one feels him ready to do an entire session.

All these lessons, well-executed, adapted to each horse's nature, perfected by the shoulder-in and the croup to the wall, followed by the straight line on the center of the *manège* (which is where each lesson should be finished in order to collect and straighten the haunches) will make, with time, a horse free, comfortable, and obedient in his canter, a gait which is as enjoyable for those watching as it is comfortable and pleasing to ride.

CHAPTER XVII

*On Voltes, Half-Voltes, Passades, Pirouettes,
& the* Terre-A-Terre

FIRST ARTICLE

On Voltes

The old trainers created the voltes to make their horses more clever in sword and pistol fights, and they were used a great deal before suspension of the duel fights. One concentrated on producing great obedience and speed on the circle to make the horse more agile and quick in turning the croup, in order to overtake the enemy's croup, or to avoid having his own overtaken by always keeping head-to-head with his adversary. Afterwards, this exercise was also made into a movement on a course where one still surrounded the haunches in order to demonstrate the rider's knowledge and the horse's skill. This is why two types of voltes are accepted: those that are used in combat and those that are done for enjoyment on a course.

In the voltes which are used in combat, a horse must never be taken onto a square or onto two tracks because, in this posture, one would not be able to overtake the enemy's croup. This must be done on a round track with only half of a haunch kept to the inside, so that the horse is more secure on his hindquarters. Since the weapons are held in the right hand which, for this reason, is called the *sword hand,* a combat horse must be very supple on the right side, because it is rare to change hands unless dealing with a left-handed person.

As for the voltes seen in the school movements, they must be done on two tracks, on a square whose four corners are rounded with the shoulders, which is called *embracing the volte.* This exercise on two tracks is taken from the croup to the wall, a lesson which is followed by making a horse do voltes in reverse which, as a rule, aid in properly executing ordinary voltes.

Thus, when a horse has become obedient in both directions with the croup to the wall for the length of the wall, one must (by reversing the shoulder in each corner of the school) continue to keep the horse in this posture for the length of the four walls until he freely obeys in both directions.

One must then reduce the long square formed by the four walls of the school into a narrow square (as is shown in the diagram), by keeping the head and the shoulders toward the center and by reversing or, rather, stopping the shoulders at the end of each line of the square (in other words, in each corner) in order that the haunches can overtake the other line.

Even though the head and shoulders of a horse that is being trotted on the longe or enlarged on circles with the croup to the outside may be toward the center, one must not assume that these are circles-in-reverse (as some riders wrongly assume). There is a big difference because, when one puts a horse on circles with the head to the inside and the croup to the outside, it is the inside legs which are enlarging or, in other words, which pass over the outside legs, as in the lesson we have given for preparing the horse for the shoulder-in; however, in the case of the volte-in-reverse, it is the outside legs which must pass and *"chevaler"* over the inside ones, as in the croup to the wall, which is much more difficult for a horse to do because he is more collected and on his haunches in this posture. This is also why one does not ask him for this movement until he has begun to understand the hand and the legs well and he moves sideways easily.

The entire problem with the volte-in-reverse is in bending the horse in the direction in which he is going to make the shoulders lead and to be able to stop them in the four corners of the square, thereby putting the haunches on another line. The horse should have no problem in easily executing this in a short while if he has already been made supple and obedient in the croup to the wall. One must return to the lesson if he resists in the narrow square in which a horse must be enclosed in order to accomplish what is called *volte-in-reverse.*

As soon as the horse freely obeys on two tracks and in both directions on the wide and narrow squares as well as in the volte-in-reverse lesson, one must place him on an ordinary volte, keeping his croup toward the center and the head and shoulders toward the wall (at a distance of two or three feet), so that the shoulders describe the larger square and the croup (being toward the center), the smaller square. Each corner must be rounded by the shoulders, while actively carrying and turning the head onto the other line and while keeping the haunches in a steady posture when one turns the forehand; however, the track of the haunches must be made entirely square. While thus carrying a horse sideways, from corner to corner, he is never leaning or stiff on the volte. This last fault is serious because it disables the horse's haunches and ruins his hocks. These are problems which some horsemen attribute to voltes in general, but it is, without a doubt, the stiff and fixed voltes which we are speaking of, since I do not believe a sensitive rider can say the same for an air which makes a horse's obedience and gracefulness so evident, which

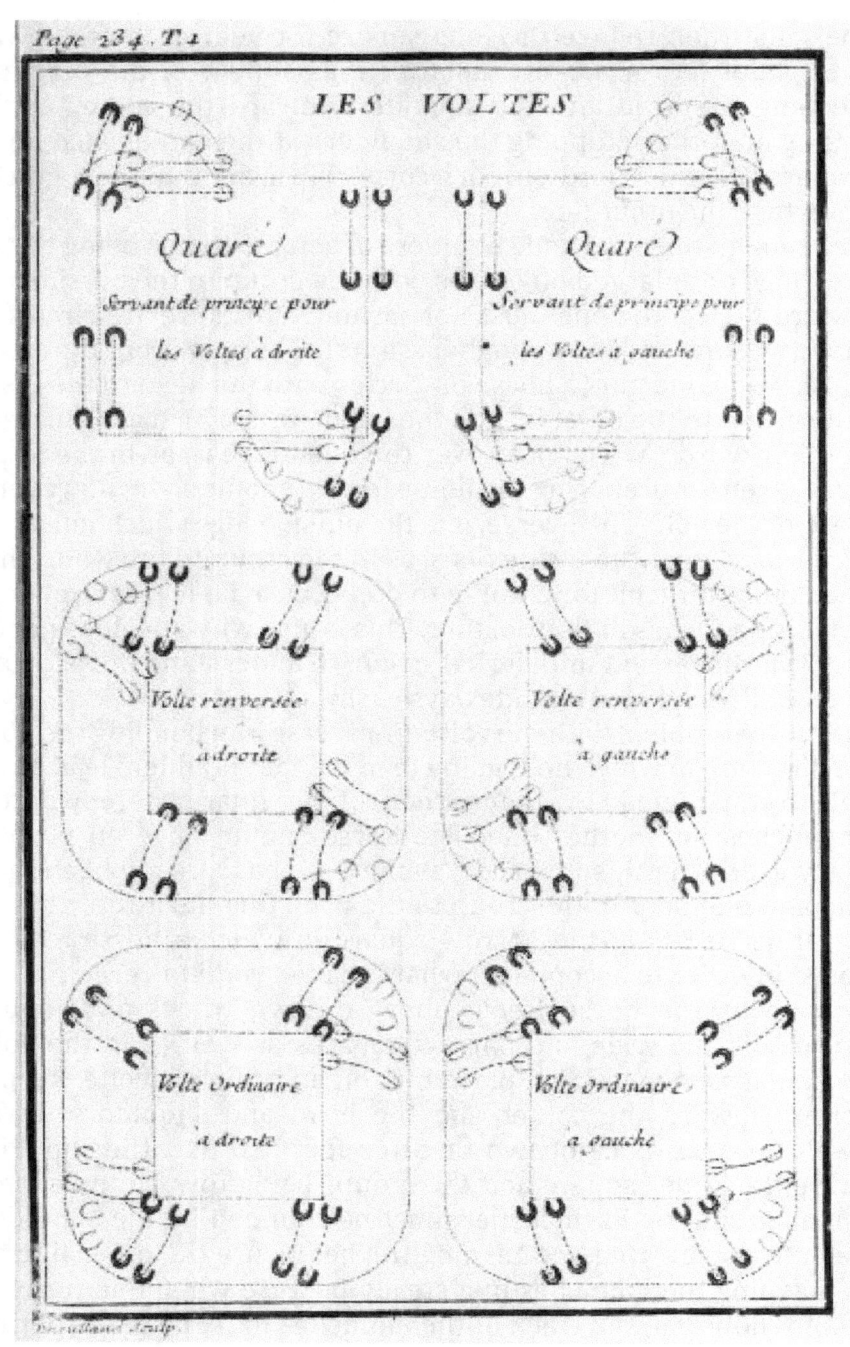

Legend
Les Voltes - The Voltes
Quaré - Square
Servant de Principe pour les Voltes - Used as a Rule
for the Voltes
Volte Renversée — Reverse Volte
Volte Ordinaire — Ordinary Volte
Directions: *à droite* - to the right
à gauche - to the left

beautifies his action, and gives endless grace to a rider who executes this movement well.

The knowledgeable de la Broue, who was the first to find the precision and the proportions of the nice voltes, still gives an excellent lesson for preparing a horse for this air. It is to take the horse at the school walk, straight and on a single track, on the four lines of the square with the head placed to the inside; and (at the end of each line), when the haunches have reached the angle formed by the meeting of the other line, to turn the shoulders until they have reached the line of the haunches (as can be seen in the diagram). This lesson is so effective that it keeps a horse straight between the legs and it gives him much suppleness in the shoulders. The steps on a straight line rid him of the chance to resist and back up, and the rounding of the shoulders (at the end of each line of the square) teaches a horse to turn easily; the haunches, while remaining steady and bent in this movement, are working to support the action of the outside shoulder and forearm. Practicing these rules for the square in consideration of the horse's nature (by keeping the one that leans or pulls on the hand on a straight line, by chasing forward the one that resists, and by activating the shoulders of both in each corner) will adjust, little by little, and without violence, the head, the neck, the shoulders, and the haunches of a horse while he is only barely aware of the constraint of this lesson.

In order to be able to easily turn the shoulders and to prevent the haunches from escaping at the end of each line of the square, it is necessary to half-halt before turning the forehand; and, after the half-halt, it is necessary to activate the hand so that the free action of the shoulders is not prevented. Also, the horse must be bent in the direction that he is moving, so that he carries the head, the bend, and the movement together on the track and when rounding each corner of the volte. When the horse has become obedient in this lesson at the collected school walk, one must make him execute it at an animated and elevated passage and then make him practice it at the canter, always in the same posture (in other words, straight in the shoulders and in the haunches and bent in the direction he is going). Each short lesson, be it at the passage or the canter, must end in the center of the volte by turning the horse in the middle of a line of the square, by moving him forward to the center, and stopping him straight between the legs, after which he is given his head.

Once the horse will passage freely on one track on four lines of the square and has achieved the ease of a collected canter in the same posture and in a nice bend in both directions, one must then make him passage on two tracks, taking note (as we have mentioned several times and which cannot be overly emphasized) to make the shoulders lead in order to give the shoulder outside the volte ease in passing the outside forearm over the inside, which is the biggest difficulty because, by holding back the free movement of the shoulders, the horse would be leaning and stiff in the volte. It is, nevertheless, necessary to keep the haunches more constrained and behind for horses who lean or pull on the hand in order to make them lighter in the forehand. It is not necessary, in this case, that the croup move before the shoulders. On the other hand, those that are lighter and less strong must not be so confined in the haunches so that they can move more freely while still being kept in a free, forward action.

One must not be too precise when first working a horse on the voltes because the horse that is naturally impatient will become worried enough to cause much disorder, and the horse that is lazy and in a sluggish mood will have his energy and his courage dulled. One must also not start with voltes for a horse who has been out of work for a few days; since he is feeling too good, he will use his back to resist. These types of horses must be lengthened at the canter on one track until they are no longer feeling good and have relaxed their back. This is why a knowledgeable rider will take care to stop working on precision to this degree and will return to the first rules at the slightest problem.

One must passage a horse for quite a while on the two-track circles before cantering him in this posture, and, when one feels him supple and comfortable, he will (with very little animation) assume, on his own, an active, shortened, and flowing on-the-haunches canter which is the true canter for the voltes.

What are called "redoubled voltes" are those that are made many times, one after another, in the same direction; but it is necessary that a horse has acquired much freedom, is of good wind, and understands the precise proportions of this exercise well before making him redouble in the voltes because too severe a lesson would confuse his spirit and his energy. This is why it is necessary, in the beginning, when finishing each volte, to stop and praise him a little in order to reassure his memory and his strength and to give him time to catch his breath. One must also change direction and place to rid him of the apprehension which this constraint would cause him.

The changes of direction on the circles are done in two ways; sometimes to the outside, sometimes to the inside.

In order to change direction to the outside of the volte, one must only place the head and bend it in the other direction and, by making the horse move away from the inside leg (which thus becomes the outside leg), he will have changed direction.

The change of direction inside of the volte is done by turning the horse on one of the middle lines of the square, then by taking him forward on a straight line toward the center of the volte, and next by putting him sideways until reaching the other line in order to place him and assume the other direction. When this last change of direction begins and ends with the haunches-in, it is called *half-volte inside the volte.*

As for the size of a volte, it must be adjusted to a horse's height and length because a small horse on a large square or a large horse on a small square would not be graceful. Horsemen have found an accurate size by using the space of two horses' lengths from one track to another of the hind feet, so that the diameter of a regular volte must be made up of four horses' lengths.

ARTICLE II

On the Half-Voltes

The half-volte is a narrow change of direction with the haunches to the inside which is done either on the volte, as we have just stated, or at the end of a straight line. A half-volte must be made up of three lines; in the first, one makes a horse move sideways for a distance of twice his length (without moving forward or back); one then turns his shoulders onto a second line of equal length and, after having turned onto the third line, one carries the horse slightly forward and closes the half-volte by having the four legs arrive on the line of the wall in the other direction. It is necessary that a horse's four legs (when finishing the half-volte) arrive on the same line because otherwise the half-volte would be open with the hind end enlarged and away from the track of the front feet; the horse would thus resume moving forward with only the inside haunch and not with both haunches, which would make him throw himself onto the shoulders. It is thus necessary, at the end of each change of direction or of each half-volte, that the horse be straight so that he can use his two haunches together to chase the forehand and make it light.

Before beginning a half-volte, it is necessary to half-halt with the balance kept a little behind so that the horse places himself on the haunches. The end of the lesson must not be weak or dis- united, but rather as energetic and distinct as the horse's nature will permit, so that the half-volte is accomplished with an equal amount of expression, accuracy, and energy.

It is not at all necessary to do the half-voltes with a horse who does not already know how to freely passage on the entire volte because, in a smaller space, he would be crowded and confined, which would never happen if he had been confirmed in a passage on one track, animated and elevated, on the four lines of the square of the volte. When the horse is sluggish or resists, one must chase him forward and, similarly, if he throws himself too much on the hand and the shoulders, he must be backed. Once he has obeyed at the passage on the half-volte, one must animate him at the end of the third line, in order to make him do four or

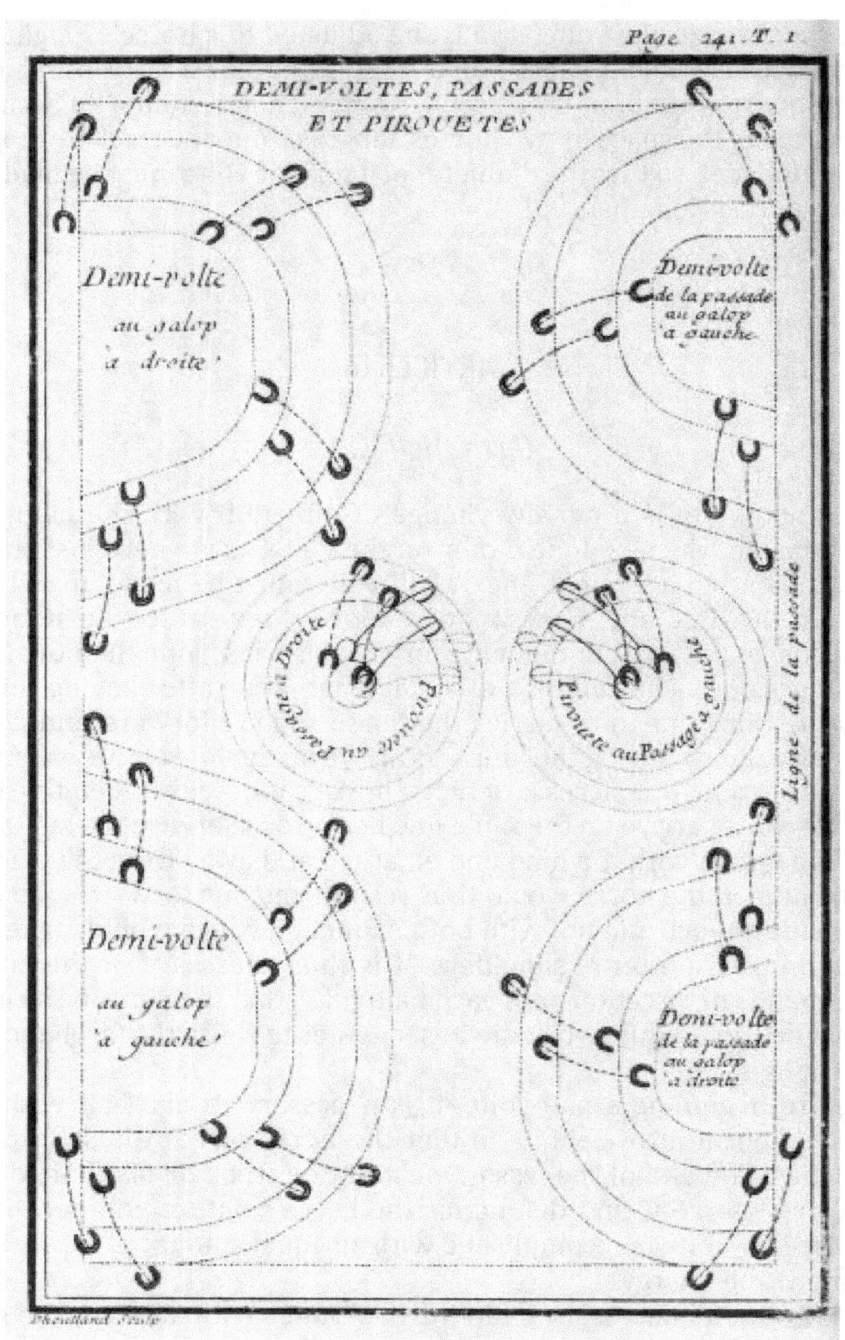

Legend
Demi-Volte au Galop à ... - Half-Volte at Canter to the ...
Passade Demi-Volte au Galop à ... - Passade Half-Volte at Canter to the
Pirouette au Passage à ... - Pirouette at Passage to...
Ligne de la Passade - Track of the Passade
Directions: *à droite* - to the right & *à gauche* - to the left
de la passade - from the passade
& *Ligne de la Passade* - line of the passade

five beats of a canter which is collected, low, and active; one must then praise him and, when one feels that he is well prepared, one must begin and end the half-volte at the canter.

The order of the lesson must be varied often, as much for the voltes as for the half-voltes, by changing direction and location because if one were to always do the half-voltes in the same place, the horse, anticipating the rider's will, would want to do them by himself.

If it happens that the horse resists the size and precision of the voltes and half-voltes, he must be put back into the shoulder-in and the croup to the wall; in this way his anger will pass and his spirit will be lessened. However, these problems only happen to those riders who do not follow nature and who want to push the horses and train them too quickly. On the other hand, they must be made to progress through ease and suppleness and not through violence because the more that a horse becomes supple and understands the rider's will, the more he will want only to obey unless his nature is absolutely rebellious. In this case, one must not ask him for any of the regular movements but only for a simple obedience, which will allow one to determine a use for him which is in accord with his disposition.

ARTICLE III

On Passades

The passade, as we have explained in the chapter on the artificial movements, is a straight line on which a horse passes and re-passes (which is why it is called *Passade*), and it is at the two ends of this line that one does a change of hand or a half-volte.

The line of the passade must be about five horses' lengths and the half-voltes must only be one horse's length in width, so that they are narrower than half of a regular half-volte because, since this movement is used in combat, the sooner a rider can turn his horse after giving a blow of the sword to his enemy, the sooner he will be ready to strike another blow. These types of half-voltes are done in three beats, and the last beat must close the half-volte. A horse must be collected and on the haunches when turning in order to be steadier on his back feet and to avoid slipping; the rider is thus also more comfortable and *deeper* in the saddle.

There are two types of passades. There are those that are done at the collected canter, as much on the lines of the passade as on the half-voltes; and there are those that are called *"furieuses"* (furious) where one leaps with all legs at once from the middle of the straight line to the spot where one indicates the halt to begin the half-volte. Thus, in the "furious" passades, after having finished the half-volte, one continues at a collected canter until reaching the middle of the straight line, as much to steady oneself in the saddle as to observe the enemy's movements (which one escapes by departing at great speed and then collecting the horse for the other direction).

Once the horse is obedient at the passades along the wall and changes leads easily (without becoming disunited) at the end of each half-volte, one must be able to do them outside the school in order to be able to meet the enemy.

One also does passades where the half-voltes are as wide as the regular half-voltes. Thus, it is no longer a combat movement but a school movement which is done for enjoyment or to enlarge a horse who is overly tight. Similarly, one also makes the line of the passade longer or shorter, depending upon whether the horse is throwing himself on the hand or holding himself back, in order to always keep him attentive to the action of the rider's legs and hand.

Even though this movement is as beautiful as it is difficult to execute, we will not go into much detail, since the same rules are used as for the voltes (which we have just explained). If the horse refuses to obey, this is due either to a bad disposition or to a problem of suppleness and obedience, in which case a return to the principles that we have established is necessary.

ARTICLE IV

On The Pirouette

A pirouette is no more than a volte within the horse's length without changing place; the haunches remain in the center and the shoulders make the circle. In this action, the inside hind leg is not raised at all but rather turns in one place and serves as a pivot around which the three other legs and the horse's body turn.

The half-pirouette is a half-volte in one place and within the horse's length; it is a type of change of hand which is done by turning a horse from the head to the tail with the haunches remaining in the same place.

The passades and the pirouettes, as well as the voltes and the half-voltes, are combat movements which are used for prompt turning to avoid being taken by surprise, to anticipate the enemy, to avoid his attack, or to attack him more diligently.

There are few horses who can do several pirouettes in a row of equal size (which is the beauty of this air) because few horses have the qualities needed for this exercise. These qualities are being very free in the shoulders and being very secure on the haunches. For example, those who have a head, neck, and shoulders which are overly fleshy are not good for this exercise.

Before a horse is activated at the canter in the pirouettes, he must be made to do some half-pirouettes at the walk in each direction (sometimes in one place, sometimes in another) and, to the extent that he obeys without problems, the rider should collect him in the passage and ask him for entire pirouettes so that (without disturbing the haunches) the head and the shoulders will be, upon finishing the pirouette, in the spot where they began. In this way, one will soon be able to easily do them at the canter.

If, after having been made sufficiently supple and obedient, a horse resists in the air, this is proof that his haunches are not good enough to support the entire forehand and the rider's weight; but, if he has the necessary qualities, he will, in time, do as many pirouettes as the rider's good judgment will allow.

In order to change direction in the pirouette, it is necessary to promptly place the head in the other direction and support the horse with the outside leg to prevent the croup from leaving the canter. However, it is not necessary that the horse be as bent in this air as on the ordinary volte because, if the head were too much to the inside, the croup would leave the center while doing the pirouette.

The pirouettes are varied according to the horse's disposition; at times one does some in the middle of a change of direction without interrupting the order of the lesson, which continues as usual. However, what truly shows a horse's obedience and accuracy is, while working on the voltes, to narrow a horse little by little until he has reached the center of the volte and then to make him do, all in one breath, as many pirouettes as his strength and his wind will permit.

ARTICLE V

On the Terre-a-Terre

According to The Duke of Newcastle's definition, which is very accurate, the "*terre-a-terre*" is a canter in two beats and on two tracks. It is more shortened and collected than the ordinary canter, and the position of the feet is different in that a horse raises the two front legs together and places them back on the ground together; the back legs accompany the front in the same movement, which makes a low, quick cadence where the horse marks time with a refrain of the haunches which leave the ground with a great force. In order to have a clearer idea, one must imagine this air as being a series of small, very low jumps with the horse always going slightly forward and to the side. Since, in this posture, the haunches do not move as far forward under the belly as at the canter, this is what makes the action quicker, lower, and more decided.

It is still necessary to notice that, in the *"terre-a-terre,"* the horse is leaning more on the outside legs than the inside, which are more forward and begin the track (but not as much as in the canter); and, since the croup is very constrained in an air which is so hurried and swift in the haunches, the horse will be more enlarged in front than behind, which places the outside shoulder slightly back and gives freedom to the inside shoulder.

It is easy to believe (because of the constraint in which this air keeps the horse) that this exercise is nevertheless severe and that few horses are capable of executing it with all the necessary precision and clearness. A horse must be very muscular and supple to be asked for this movement. Those whose lightness and spirit is not matched by strength and experience fear the constraint of such desired rules; also, the true horsemen view this movement, which has become very rare, as the means by which the rider's knowledge and the horse's skill may be shown.

One must not fall into the error of those who indifferently give the name of *"terre-a-terre"* to the gait of those horses that drag along in a bad canter which is low to the ground and has no swift action to press their haunches into the fast and active cadence. It is the refrain of this active cadence which makes the difference between the *"terre-a-terre"* and the bad canter evident. Often, due to a lack of knowledge regarding the true definition of each movement's air, one is not in a position to judge the horse's capabilities or, consequently, to give him an air which suits his disposition. This error, of thus confusing the airs which are the ornaments of the beautiful movements, results in giving some riders (whose capabilities rely largely upon routine) a pretended knowledge which exists only in their ill-founded self-sufficiency and in the blind admiration of those that lecture them without any knowledge of the cavalry art.

Since the perfection of the *"terre-a-terre"* consists in having the outside haunch compressed, it is necessary, in the voltes in the air, that the square be even more perfect than those which are done at the simple canter on two tracks. However, one must be careful in the corners that the inside hind leg does not precede the shoulders because the horse, thus being too enlarged in the haunches, would be stiffened and, by forcing the rider's hand to pull him from this false position, could give a leap forward. One must also be careful that the hand is not too high because the horse would not be able to move low and quickly, nor flow equally fast.

The most usual mistakes made by a horse while working in the *"terre-a-terre"* are to back up, to raise the forehand too much, or to drag the haunches. When some of these problems arise, it is necessary to bring the horse forward with the spurs in order to correct him, to tell him to keep himself more together, and to activate his cadence more. Since, in this exercise, the parts of the horse are really worked, one must always feel what the state of the horse's state of obedience is (in regard to his strength and his spirit) in order to finish the lesson before weariness gives him a reason to fight back.

The rules for training a horse in the *"terre-a-terre"* are taken from one's knowledge of his nature and what one finds his attitude to be for this air. This one will easily know when (after having suppled him according to the rules) he assumes on his own (when collected) the refrain of the haunches that we have just mentioned. He thus will, without a doubt, have the disposition for executing this movement, but it is necessary to spare his strength, especially in the beginning, by only asking him for four half-voltes in a row at the most, which he will easily do if he has been prepared by the principles which must guide him in this lesson. To the degree that his strengths and his wind will make him more supple and alert, one will be able (after having done four half-voltes, in other words, two in each direction) to relax him at the slow and measured collected canter, in order to next collect him on the square in the middle of the area and to put him back in two or three voltes of his air, and then finish and give him his head.

CHAPTER XVIII

On the Airs above the Ground

We have said that all the leaps which are more elevated than the *"terre-a-terre"* and are used in the good schools are called the *High Airs.* There are seven of them, namely the *Pesade,* the *Mézair,* the *Courbette,* the *Croupade,* the *Ballotade,* the *Capriole,* and the *Pas-et-ie-Saut* (the step and jump).

Before entering into detail on the rules pertaining to each of these airs, it seems appropriate to me to examine what type of nature a horse must have to be chosen for this use, what qualities are necessary to endure the strain of the leaps, and which dispositions are not at all suited.

A horse must have a natural inclination and show himself in some air to make a good jumper; otherwise, one would be wasting his time and would shock and ruin the horse instead of training him. An error which is overly common is to believe that great strength is necessary for a jumper. This excessive vigor, which certain horses have, makes them stiff and inept and makes them do leaps and disorganized movements which exhaust them, causing discomfort to the rider (because these disorganized and disorderly leaps usually are accompanied by violent efforts which are indicative of the horse's malice). A horse with this type of character must be confined to the pillars where a continuous routine of school leaps will punish him sufficiently for his bad nature. A horse who is gifted with moderate strength and who has much courage and lightness is incomparably better, because he gives what he can out of willingness and will sustain his exercise for a long time. On the other hand, the one that has much strength and unwillingness will be exhausted before being trained, due to the extreme means which must be used to master his rebelliousness. In addition, one will find certain horses who, with somewhat weak haunches, cannot become acceptable jumpers because they prefer leaving the ground to putting their weight on their haunches.

The horse that is referred to as having good force is the one who is sinewy and light, who naturally distributes his strength evenly and gracefully, who accepts the bit with a light and made mouth, who has strong limbs, free shoulders, good fetlocks, pasterns and feet, and who is willing.

Horses whose dispositions are not at all suited to the high airs are those that are overly sensitive, impatient and short-tempered, who easily become hot and anxious, tighten up, stamp the ground, and refuse to elevate themselves. There are others who, due to malice and cowardice, rebel when approached, resulting in disorderly leaps which give proof of their vice and their desire to throw their rider to the ground. There are still others who drag because of sore or defective feet, and, upon landing, the pain prevents them from doing another leap. Those that have a false mouth and poor contact almost always have the head in disorder when they descend from each leap, which is very disagreeable. Thus, when one finds a horse who has any of these imperfections, one must not intend, under any circumstance, to make a jumper out of him.

There is still something else to consider; that is, when one has found a horse of good strength and disposition, to know how to judge which type of leap is proper for him in order to avoid forcing him into an air which does not suit his nature or his disposition. In addition, before training him in this air, it is necessary that he have been suppled and made obedient in the lessonsfòr which we have given the principles. Let us now enter into the details of each air.

FIRST ARTICLE

On the Pesade

The *pesade,* as we have already defined it, is an air in which the horse raises the forehand quite high and in one place, keeping the back feet securely on the ground, without moving them forward or turning them. Properly speaking, the *pesade* is not an elevated air, since the hind end does not accompany the forehand (as in the other airs) and does not leave the ground. But since one uses this lesson in order to teach a horse to lightly raise the forehand, to gracefully bend the forearms, and to affirm him on his haunches in order to prepare him for leaping with more freedom, one places the *pesade* at the head of all the high airs as being the foundation and the first rule. Moreover, one uses the *pesade* in order to correct the faults of those who, in the airs of the *mézair* and *courbette,* pound the dust by working too close to the ground and by shuffling their front legs in their air. It is also for this reason that, at the end of a line of *courbettes,* it is customary to make the last one high in the forehand and in one place, which is nothing other than the *pesade* which one does, not only to be graceful in stopping, but moreover to maintain lightness in the forehand.

The *pesade* must not be confused with the uneven beat made by horses who rear, even though these horses also raise the forehand very high and leave the hind end on the ground. The difference between the two is very great. In the action made by a horse when he raises himself in the *pesade,* he must be in the hand and have the haunches and the hocks bent underneath himself, which prevents him from raising the forehand higher than is necessary. At the peak of a rear, the horse is rigidly stretched on the hocks, off the hand, and in danger of flipping over.

One must not, under any circumstance, make a horse do *pesades* who has not been suppled in the shoulders, made obedient to the hand and the legs, or is not confirmed in the piaffe; but when he has achieved this degree of obedience, one animates him with the long whip in the pillars, by lightly touching him with the switch on the front legs and in time with when he brings himself forward into the ropes and brings the haunches underneath himself. For however little he raises himself, one must stop him and praise him, and to the degree that he obeys, one must touch him more actively so that he raises the forehand higher.

Since, in all the high airs, a horse must bend the forearms so that the feet tuck up almost to the elbow (which makes the horse very graceful), it is necessary to correct the unsightly action of those who, instead of bending the knees, stretch the legs forward by crossing the feet one over the other. This fault, which is called *jouer de l'épinette,* is easy to correct by punishment with the switch or the whip and by using one or the other strongly on his knees and his fetlock. Another fault is when a horse raises himself on his own accord without being asked. The punishment for these horses is to make them kick. Thus a fault is corrected by its opposite, and to avoid his continuing with this problem, each lesson must be started with the piaffe, then one must ask the horse for some *pesade,* and finish with the piaffe. This variety in the lesson will make a horse attentive to following his rider's will.

Once the horse easily obeys the air of the *pesade* in the pillars, it is then necessary to ride him and, while passaging him at liberty, ask him for one or two *pesades* in place without his crossing over and, after the last, to move two or three steps forward. If, when returning the front feet to the ground, he leans or pulls on the hand, one must back him, then raise him in a *pesade* and pat him if he obeys. If, on the other hand, he resists or backs up instead of raising the forehand, one must chase him forward and, when he is moving well, indicate a half followed by *a pesade,* which is done by compressing him a little. Since the wiser horses always show some anger when one begins to ask them for the high airs, one must not ask them for as much of their air as they can give, because they will become stiff, lose the habit of easily turning, and even use their air to fight back by raising themselves when one does not ask them for it. Thus, one must, in the beginning, treat them with much caution and be careful that they do not fall into any of these bad habits, which could make them awkward to deal with.

ARTICLE II

On the Mézair

The *mézair*, as was well defined by some riding masters, is nothing more than a half-courbette whose movement is less elevated, lower, quicker, and more forward than the true courbette, but also more elevated and measured than the *"terre-a-terre."*

In the pillars, it is easy to see if a horse is more inclined for the *mézair* than for any other leap, because if, by nature, he is more inclined toward this air (when one asks him for it), he will assume, on his own, a cadence which is more elevated than the *"terre-a-terre"* and quicker than the courbette. When, through several repetitive lessons, one becomes aware of his disposition, one must confirm him in this air by using the same rules as for the *pesades;* in other words, to begin each short lesson with the piaffe, followed by some beats of the *mézair* by using the switch on the forehand and the long whip on the hind end and *so* on, alternately. When one decides he is ready to practice this lesson at liberty, one must, after having passaged him on one track, collect him to make him move in his air (be it on the change of direction or on the half-volte) and always on two tracks, because moving on one track is not used for the *mézair* or the *"terre-à-terre."*

The most useful and graceful aids which are used for putting a horse in the *mézair* are to touch him lightly and carefully with the switch on the outside shoulder while aiding and rousing him with the calves. When the croup does not accompany the forehand enough, one crosses the switch under the hand in order to touch the croup, which makes the hind end have a quicker and stronger beat.

If the horse falls into the usual faults of almost all horses that are trained in the high airs (which are to resist, to throw themselves too much on the hand, or to work without waiting for the rider's aids), one must use the above remedies with the judgement, care, and patience which are necessary in a horseman.

In this air, one must still observe the same proportions as in the *"terre-a-terre"* (in other words, keeping the horse in the precise space of the voltes and the half-voltes) because, since these airs have much in common and form a tight, swift movement, the horse's posture must be the same in these two airs.

The courbette

ARTICLE III

On the Courbette

The *courbette* is a leap which is more elevated in the forehand and more measured and sustained than the *mézair*. At the instant that the front legs return to the ground, the haunches must beat down and accompany the forehand with a cadence which is even, swift, and low. Thus the difference between the *mézair* and the *courbette* is that in the *mézair* the horse's forehand is lower to the ground and he advances and activates the cadence of his air more than in the *courbette;* in the *courbette* he is more elevated and more sustained in the forehand, and he beats the haunches down with more constraint by keeping the forehand in the air for a longer period of time. One must take note that in the canter, the *"terre-a-terre,"* and the pirouette the horse carries his legs one in front of the other, as much in the forehand as the hind-end. However, in the *mézair,* the *courbette,* and all the other high airs, they must be equal and one should not advance more than the other when they are on the ground, which would be a great fault that is called *dragging the haunches.*

Besides the natural disposition which a horse must have to do the *courbettes* well, much skill is always necessary in order to start him and confirm him in this air which is, of all those that are called high airs, the most popular and the most used. The reason is that this is a graceful leap in a movement which, without being severe, proves the good quality of a horse's haunches and shows the rider in a pleasing posture. This air was formerly very much in use amongst the cavalry officers who prided themselves on having well-trained horses, be it at the head of their troup or on the parade days. One would see them, from time to time, break off into some pretty *courbettes,* which served as much to animate a horse (when the loftiness of his step slackened) as to keep him obedient and to then give him a more elevated, proud, and light step.

One must not ask a horse for *courbettes* who is not obedient in the *"terre-a-terre"* and in the *mézair,* because a good *"terre-a-terre"* and a true *mézair* are more than halfway to arriving at the *courbette* (in the instance that a horse has the disposition for going in this air). Those that are not suited are the horses who are lazy, heavy, or resist through malice, and, similarly, those that are impatient, worried, fiery, and spirited; because all the elevated airs increase the natural anger of these types of horses, make them lose their memory, and destroy their obedience. Thus, the one that is destined to this exercise is sinewy, light, and hardy and, along with this, intelligent, quiet, and obedient.

When, with these qualities, one sees, in the pillars, that a horse's favorite air is the *courbette,* it is necessary (after having taught him to elevate the forehand well by means of the *pesades)* to then animate the haunches with the long whip, making him press the croup down and lower the forehand so that he can assume the precise cadence and the true posture of his air. When he has become regulated to some degree and when he can do four or five *courbettes* in a row without problems and according to the rules, it is necessary to make him do some at liberty on the centerline of the *manège* and not along the wall; because the horses that become accustomed to elevating themselves along the wall are only moving out of habit and have problems when one asks them for the same thing elsewhere. In the beginning, one must not ask for several *courbettes* in a row; rather, by passaging and piaffing a horse on the straight line, when one feels that he is well collected and has a good contact, one steals two or three of them from him which are well above the ground and well measured. One then continues with some steps of passage and one finishes with two or three beats of piaffe because, if it happens that one finishes the last beat with a *courbette,* the horse will use this air to fight back.

    In order to aid a horse well in the *courbettes,* the timing of the hand must be prompt and agile in order to raise the forehand; the rider's legs must follow the beat of the *courbettes* without overly pressing for it, because a horse will naturally assume his proper beat and cadence when he begins to adjust himself. One must certainly not stiffen the legs because by aiding the horse too much with them, the horse would be overly hurried. On the contrary, one must be supple from the knees to the stirrups and have the point of the foot slightly low, which loosens the tendons. The only movement on the horse, when one maintains the balance in a straight and comfortable posture, is that of the calves aiding the horse without being closed (unless the horse is resisting; in which case one must use his aids more vigorously and then relax them).

    The *courbettes* must be adjusted to the horse's nature: the one that has too much contact with the bit should be encouraged to make them shorter and more sustained on the haunches; and the one that resists must be more forward in them. Otherwise, the former would become too heavy and would fight the hand, and the latter would become stiff. In order to cure these faults, one often puts the horses in a shoulder-in in the passage; this lesson will keep them as free as they should be so they can easily obey during this air.

    When a horse freely obeys (and without crossing over) on the straight line in the *courbettes,* it is necessary (in order to prepare him for doing the *voltes* in the air) to put him on the square we have given as a rule for the voltes at the canter. And, when one feels him to be straight in the passage and in balance with the heels on the four lines of the square, it is necessary from time to time, to have him do some *courbettes,* except in the corners of the square. Here one must not raise him, but rather freely turn the shoulders onto the other line without the croup becoming disorganized; because if one were to raise him while turning, he would stiffen and back up.

When he executes this lesson well on the four lines and is advanced enough and has enough wind to do the whole square in *courbettes,* one can begin to teach him to do them with the haunches to the inside. For this, one must passage him with the croup to the wall and, in this posture, have him do one or two *courbettes* on two tracks. The *courbettes* are not done by aiding the horse when he is in the air, but rather when his front feet return to the ground. Then one aids him with the outside leg in order to carry him sideways for a beat; then a *courbette* with the two calves while supporting him with the hand; and so on, a step sideways followed by a *courbette.*

When the horse goes well with the croup to the wall, one must place him on the square in the middle of the arena and, while keeping him on two tracks, accustom him to raising himself in his air in this posture, while keeping the severity of this lesson in accord with his obedience and his disposition. One must not keep the haunches as much to the inside on the voltes at the *courbette* as at the *"terre-a-terre"* and the *mézair* because if the croup was too constrained he would not be able to beat the haunches down as freely. This is why only a little more than half a haunch must be kept to the inside. Also, one must not bend a horse as much on the voltes at the *courbette* as at the canter or the *"terre-a-terre."* He must only have one eye looking to the inside of the volte. And when he does *courbettes* on a straight line and on one track, he must not be bent at all but, rather, straight in the head, shoulders, and haunches.

Aside from the *courbettes* on the voltes, there are still two other ways of doing them, which are the *courbettes in a cross* and the *courbettes in a row.*

In order to accustom a horse to doing the *courbettes in a cross,* one must passage the horse on one track on the straight line (for about four horses' lengths), back him afterwards on the same line, then return to the middle of the straight line; afterwards, carry him sideways on the right heel (for about two horses' lengths), then sideways on the left heel (again two lengths) to the middle of the straight line; one finally returns, sideways on the right heel, to finish on the middle of the line, where one stops and praises him. When a horse has learned how to passage on these lines (without crossing over) forward, back, and to the side on one and then the other heel, one does a *courbette* at the beginning, middle, and end of each line. And if, after several lessons, the horse does not resist at all, one attempts to make him do the entire cross in *courbettes.* When one raises him while backing, it is not necessary that the body be back, but straight, and even slightly forward (without this being evident) in order to give more freedom to the croup. It is when the front feet return to the ground (and not when the horse is in the air) that one must aid him by holding him with the hand so that he takes one step back without raising his body; one then does a *courbette,* and so on in this manner.

In the *courbettes in a row,* one does two *courbettes* going forward, as many to the rear, two others to the side on one heel, and then the other; and thus, one after another, forward, to the side, and back, indiscriminately and without observing the proportions on the ground (as in the cross). One makes the horse do, all in one breath, as much as his disposition and his strength will permit. However, a rider must have mastered his aids well, and the horse must have mastered his aids well, and the horse must be well adjusted and very sinewy in order to execute these movements of the cross and the row in *courbettes* with the grace and the freedom that he must have. One must note that these movements have disappeared from our time.

ARTICLE IV

On the Croupade and the Ballotade

The *Croupade* and the *Ballotade* are two airs which only differ from each other in regard to the position of the hind legs.

In the *croupade,* when the horse's four legs are in the air, he tucks and withdraws the hind legs and feet under his belly without his irons showing. And, in the *ballotade,* when he is at the height of his jump, he shows his hind feet as if he wanted to kick; however, he does not kick out as is done in the *caprioles.*

We have already said that, for the horses destined to the high airs, the art does not suffice to produce these different positions of their legs in their jumps. Along with attention to the art and the horse's natural disposition, the limits of nature determine the rules which must be followed, in order to adjust the horses and make them gracefully execute these difficult movements.

It is always in the pillars that a horse's air must first be perceived. Those that want to begin by training a jumper at freedom without having suppled or adjusted him at the piaffe, and without having studied his air in the pillars, are making a mistake; because every jumper, besides his natural disposition for leaving the ground, must have a perfect knowledge of the hand and the legs, in order to know how to jump lightly and in the hand, as demanded and not from whim or habit.

Once a horse does some *caprioles* or *ballotades* easily and without anger in the pillars and in accord with the rider's will, one must then ask the horse for some of them at liberty by following the same order as for the above airs (especially that for the *courbettes).* One must take note that the higher the airs, the more force a horse must use to do them and that the great art is to conserve his courage and his lightness by asking him for few jumps (especially in the beginning). When he has willingly given his air a few times, he must be praised and let down.

When the horse does a straight line of *courbettes* or *ballotades* at liberty without crossing over, he must be prepared for raising himself in his air on the four lines which form the volte, by passaging him on the volte and removing him from it from time to time. If one feels that he will be obedient, one must profit from his good will by having him come off the ground on the four lines, except, as we have stated, in the corners where one must not raise him while turning. One must still give attention to the fact that, in the airs of the *croupade, ballotade,* and the *capriole,* one must never go on two tracks, but, rather, with only a half-haunch to the inside. Otherwise the hind end, due to being overly constrained, would not be able to accompany the action of the shoulders as easily. One must also be careful that, in the four corners of the volte, the croup does not escape when one turns the forehand on the other line. One must fix it and support it with the outside leg.

The aids for the high airs are the switch used in front by continuing to touch the outside shoulder lightly (the switch should not be used roughly, as is done by some riders who beat a horse's shoulder). In order to use the switch gracefully, the arm must be bent and the rider's shoulder raised to the height of the horse's shoulder. One also uses (as we have already explained) the switch under the hand and crossed over the croup in order to animate the haunches. The aid of delicately pinching with the spur is also excellent in the high airs when a horse does not leap high enough, because this aid, which must not be violent, raises a horse more than it moves him forward.

Even though one must not two-track when elevating a horse in the high airs, it is nevertheless necessary to put a horse in this posture as much at the passage as at the canter because, in this action, with the haunches more tightened, lowered, and constrained, the forehand is made lighter and better prepared for jumping. One must also not make the mistake of those who only seem to train their horses for making great efforts which weaken their strength. This is not the intention of the good school. On the contrary, one must maintain him in the suppleness, obedience, and precision which are taken from the true principles of the art. Otherwise the school would always be vague and confused and the uniformity of measurement which each air must have would be broken, and this is a perfection which must not be neglected.

ARTICLE V

On the Caprioles

The *Capriole* is, as we have stated in defining this air, the most elevated and perfect of all the leaps. When the horse is in the air, equally elevated in front and behind, he kicks out briskly. The hind legs, at this moment, are next to each other, and he lengthens them as far as possible. The hind feet, in this action, are raised to the height of the croup, and often the hocks snap due to the sudden and violent extension of this part. The term *capriole* is an Italian expression that the Neapolitan masters have given to this air because of its resemblance to the leap of the deer, which is called *Caprio* in Italian.

A horse which is destined to do *caprioles* must be sinewy, light, good in the hand, have an excellent mouth, large and with sinewy legs and hocks, and feet which are in perfect condition and suited for supporting this air; because, if nature did not form him hearty and light, one will be working him in vain. He will never have the gracefulness or the agility needed for a good jumper.

In order for a *capriole* to be perfect, the horse must raise the forehand and the hind end to the same height; in other words, at the height of his leap, the croup and the withers must be level, the head straight and steady, the forearms equally bent, and, with each leap, the horse must not advance more than a foot. There are some who, when leaping in *caprioles,* return the four feet together on the same place and raise themselves again with the same force and cadence; they continue as long as their vigor will permit. This movement is very rare and does not last a long time. It is called *Saut d'un terns* (leap in one beat) or *de Ferme-à-ferme* (from support to support).

In order to train a horse in *caprioles* (when one finds in him the qualities and the disposition which we have just explained), it is necessary, after having suppled the inside shoulder and taught him the heels at the passage and the canter, to make him elevate himself in *pesades* in the pillars. These must be done slowly in the beginning and be of good height in the forehand so that the horse has the time to adjust his feet and raises himself without anger. When the horse knows how to raise himself easily and high in the forehand, by bending the forearms well, one must teach him to kick out by means of the long whip. One should apply the whip when the forehand is in the air and ready to return to the ground, because if one were to use it as the horse was raising himself, the horse would rear and become stiff on his hocks. When the horse knows how to kick out vigorously with the forehand in the air, which forms the *capriole,* one must lessen little by little the number of *pesades* and increase the number of *caprioles;* and one must stop making him leap when it is evident that the horse has become fatigued because, with his courage and strength dissipated, his leaps would be no more than disorganized jumps and resistances.

When the horse has become obedient in this movement in the pillars, one must passage him at liberty and remove him for some time from his air on the straight line by aiding him with the switch on the shoulder, when the forehand begins to lower and not when it is raised (which would prevent him from accompanying it with the croup). When one uses the "*poinçon*" (the spike), one must observe the same thing; in other words, to press it on the middle of the croup when the horse's forehand is ready to lower (and for the same reason). As for the rider's legs, they must not be stiff or overly stretched, but comfortable and close to the horse. When the horse resists, one must use the calves and, sometimes, also delicately pinch him with the spur if he continues to resist. One must also, at the height of each jump, hold the horse for an instant in the hand as if he were suspended, which is called *soutenir* (to sustain).

The air of the *caprioles on the voltes* (in other words, on the square that we have proposed as a rule for the other airs) forms the most beautiful and difficult of all the movements due to the great problem involved in observing the proper proportions and in keeping the horse together in an even cadence, without his escaping in the forehand or the hind-end (which usually happens). Since the movement of the capriole is more extended and difficult than that of any other air, the ground space must be larger and less confined in order to give more energy and lightness to the leaps. Only half a haunch should be placed inside the volte, which makes this movement more accurate and perfect and the rider's seat more secure and beautiful. One must not follow each beat of the leap with the body, but rather hold oneself so that the movements one makes seem as much to beautify one's posture as to aid the horse.

The "Pas-et-le-Saut" & The "Galop-Gaillard" (Step and Jump & Strong, Vigorous Canter)

When the horses trained for caprioles begin to tire, they assume, on their own (as if to give themselves some relief) an air which has been called the *"pas-et-le-saut."* It is comprised of three beats; the first is a beat of collected canter or *"terre-a-terre";* the second, a *courbette;* and the third, a *capriole.* One can also put in this air horses who have more swiftness than force, in order to give them time to collect their strength by preparing them, through the first two movements, to elevate themselves in the capriole.

There are certain horses who interrupt their canter by doing some playful leaps, be it because they have too much back, have had too much rest, or because the rider holds them back too much. This is what

Cavalier

Cavalry Officer

is called the *galop-gaillard* (strong, vigorous canter). However, this movement must not, under any circumstance, pass for an air, because it arises from the whim of the horse who is only making his natural disposition to leap evident (when this playfulness is ordinary and not the result of too long a rest).

CHAPTER XIX

On war horses

The arts of war and riding owe to each other reciprocally many and great advantages. The first [art of war] influences the necessity of commanding the powers of a horse with certainty, and has given rise to established principles for attaining that goal: Academies have been established, under the patronage of the most illustrious princes. These principles, regularly practiced have contributed greatly to the regularity of military movements: and it will appear that every air of the *manège* is practiced in the evolutions of cavalry.

The passage, for example, gives a noble animated air to a horse, at the head of a squadron.

In teaching a horse to go to one side, you prepare him to gain ground, to either hand, and incline as occasion may require.

By the means of *voltes* one gains the croup [rear] of the enemy, and return instantly upon him.

Pirouettes, and demi-pirouettes, give facility in turning quickly, in single combat. And if the high airs should not have an advantage of that nature, they give the horse lightness and agility in leaping hedges and ditches, with ease to himself and pleasure to the rider.

It is certain, that the success of almost all military actions depends, upon the uniformity and regularity of the movements of the squadron, which can only arise from good instructions. On the contrary, disorder and want of unity, so often remarked in cavalry, arises from ill-dressed [poorly trained] and ill-managed horses.

This affinity, gave rise to a degree of emulation amongst the nobility, to acquire proficiency in the art of riding; that they might have the honor, and satisfaction, of serving their king and country, with better effect. From these glorious motives, the ancient equerries have been induced to publish rules to dress horses properly for war; and, in following their footsteps, we shall endeavor to elucidate the most approved practice. There are two points to be observed, in a horse destined for war: his qualities, and the rules which should be followed in dressing him.

A war horse should be of middling stature, from fourteen hands, to fourteen and a half, and this is the height required as standard, in all the corps of French cavalry. He must have a good mouth, carry his head steady, and be light in hand; those who require a full *appui* [contact on the reins], deceive themselves, for fatigue will make him heavy in the hand. He should have a good temper, courage, lungs, and good action; pliant and supple, be attentive to the slightest aid of the spurs, and well down upon his haunches, that he may depart at the instant, and stop firmly and easily; he must not have latent vice, for some horses will perform very well, when in constant exercise, but after laying by, or being rode by a bad horseman, they will become vicious: such horses require much attention, and they are only fit for the riding school: since it would be too much, to have to correct the horse, and to combat an enemy, at the same time.

Biting, and fighting with other horses are the most dangerous faults a war horse can have; for in combat, when the horse is animated, it is not easy to control him.

When all these qualities described are found in a horse, it will be an easy matter for a horseman to dress him to the *manège* of war, by following the rules we have laid down, to produce suppleness and obedience, that he may obey the hand and heel readily. This will be most assuredly effected, if after suppling the horse well by the trot, he is confirmed in the lesson of the shoulder-in, and the croup to the wall [haunches-out]; if he is taught to turn quickly, and with facility, upon war voltes; that is to say, upon a half circle [with] haunches in; if he is ready at going off upon the straight line of *passades*, light and easy, in collecting himself, at both ends of the line, to form demi-voltes to either hand; if he is ready and quid in executing pirouettes, and demi-pirouettes. These are the essential requisites to render a war horse supple and obedient to the aids; but another essential point must not be omitted, which is to familiarize him to the noise of arms, the smell and smoke of gun-powder, the sounds of drums, trumpets, and the movement of blades [of war] the sight of flags, colors, and such objects as can be expected in the field of battle. There are many bold horses that tremble at the first sight of such objects; and though they have good mouths, and possess sensibility, they lose all recollection of the intention of the aids, as well as chastisement, and abandon themselves to the strongest caprices, to flee the object of their apprehension. Such horses must be kept in constant exercise, for rest would renew their alarm; and this proves that the most subtle art cannot totally overcome natural defects.

Monsieur [Saloman] de la Broue says, that the shortest and most simple way to accustom a horse to fire arms, and other military noise, is to fire a pistol, or beat a drum, in the stable, every night and morning, at the time of giving the horse his oats; and, in a little time, this will make him as fond of the noise, as he was of the sound of the feed bucket.

Some horses are so very much alarmed, that they will start, prick up their ears, roll and turn up the white of their eyes, tremble and sweat with fear, keep their hay clenched in their teeth, without moving their jaws, and lastly, throw themselves upon the manger or over the bars. Yet by patience and good treatment they may be reformed.

Another mode I have often seen, and practiced is to put the horse into the pillars, where, in a short time, and without danger, he may be familiarized to those sounds and sights. Show him a pistol, and let him smell it (without firing it), play with the hammer of the pistol for many horses are afraid of the sound of the mechanism. When it is accustomed to this fire a charge from at a distance with your back turned towards the horse, and approach by degrees; burn priming, then go up to him, and let him smell it, to accustom him to the smell of powder; this done, caress him, and give him something to eat, and a little water; repeat this, until he is used to the smell and smoke; then load the pistol, and caress him. As the horse becomes used to the sound and smell, put in a greater charge, and fire nearer to him, and finally fire it from his back. With the same patience and perseverance, accustom him to drums, trumpets, colors [flags], and the clatter and fight of swords. Horses that are timid are generally weak, and those whose sight is not very good, are difficult to teach. Though, in the end, such horses may be trained [tamed], but I would not recommend their use for war.

It is not only within the narrow boundaries of the *manège* that this is to be practiced; the horses must also be frequently exercised, in the same way, in open country, and on the road, where they meet an infinite number of sources of fear, such as windmills, watermills, and wooden bridges are a great source of alarm for many horses. But if the horse is obedient to the aids of the hand and heel, and the rider knows how to give the aids appropriately, and if he has the genius and patience required, the horse will overcome these difficulties. Above all, on these occasions, care must be taken, never to beat a young horse, because, as we have stated before, the fear of blows, combined with the alarm arising from the disliked object, would overwhelm the horse and put him off completely.[19]

---

19 "In order to make horses stand the sound of firearms, the sound of drums, and all sorts of different noises, you must accustom them to the noises by degrees in the stable at feeding time; and instead of being frightened of it, the will soon come to like it as a signal for eating.
"With regard to such horses that are afraid of burning objects, begin by keeping them still, at a certain distance from some lighted straw; caress the horse; and in proportion with his fright diminishing, gradually approach the burning straw very gently, and increase the size of it. By this means he will very quickly be brought to be so familiar with it, as to walk undaunted even through it.
"As to horses that are apt to lie down in the water, if animating them and attacking them vigorously should fail to the desired effect, then break a straw bottle full of water upon their heads, let the water run into their ears, which is a thing they apprehend very much.
"All troop horses must be taught to stand quiet and still when they are shot off from [rider shooting from the saddle], to stop the moment you prefer, and not to move after firing until they are required to do it; this lesson ought especially to be observed in light troops; in short, the horse must be taught to be so cool and undisturbed, as to suffer the rider to act upon him with the same freedom as if he were on foot. Patience, coolness, and temper are the only means requisite of accomplishing this end. Begin by walking the horse gently, then stop and keep him from stirring for some time so as to accustom him by degrees not to have the least idea of moving without orders; if he does, then back him, and when you stop him and he is quite still, leave the reins quite loose.
"To accustom a horse to firearms, first put a pistol or a carabine [unloaded] in the manger with his feed; then accustom him to the sound of the lock and the pan; after which, when you are mounted, show the piece to him presenting it forwards, sometimes on one side, sometimes on the other; when he is thus far reconciled proceed to flash in the pan; after which put a small charge into the piece and so continue augmenting it by degrees to the quantity which is commonly used; if he seems uneasy walk him forward a few steps slowly and then stop, back, and caress him. Horses are often also disquieted and unsteady at the clash and drawing [of arms] and returning of swords; all which them must be familiarized with little by little, by frequency and gentleness.
"It is very expedient for all cavalry in general, but particularly for light cavalry, that their horses should be very ready and expert in leaping over ditches, hedges, gates, etc. The leaps, of whatever sort, that horses are brought to in the beginning ought to be very small ones; the riders must keep their bodies back, raise their hands a little in order to help the forehand of the horse up and be very attentive to their balance. It is best to begin at a low bar cover with furze [gorse: a spiny evergreen shrub] which pricking the horse's legs, if he does not raise himself

sufficiently prevents him from contracting a sluggish and dangerous habit of touching [the rail] as he goes over, which anything yielding and not pricking would give him a custom of doing. Let the ditches you first bring the horses to be narrow; and in this as in everything else, let the increase be made by degrees. Accustom them to come up to everything which they are to leap over, and to stand coolly at it for some time; and then to raise themselves gently up in order to form for themselves an idea of the distance. When they leap well from a standstill, then accustom them to walk gently up to the leap, and to go over it without first halting at it; after that practice is familiar to them, repeat the same in a gentle trot, and so by degrees faster and faster until at length, it is as familiar to them to leap flying on a full gallop as any other way; all of this is to be acquired with great facility by calm and soft means, without hurry.

"As horses are naturally apt to be frightened at the sight and smell of dead horses, it is advisable to habituate them to walk over and leap over carcasses of dead horses; and as they are particularly terrified at this sight, the greater gentleness ought consequently to be used.

"Horses should also be accustomed to swim, which often may be necessary upon [military] service; and if the men and horses both are not used to it, both may be frequently liable to perish in the water. A very small portion of strength is sufficient to guide a horse anywhere indeed, but particularly in the water, where they must be permitted to have their heads, and be in no way constrained in any shape.

"The unreasonable rage in Britain of cutting off all extremities from horses is in all cases a very pernicious custom. It is particularly so in regard to a troop horse's tail. It is almost incredible how much they suffer at the picket for want of it; constantly fretting and sweating kicking about and laming one another, tormented and stung off their meat, miserable and helpless; while other horses with their tails intact brush off all flies, are cool and at ease and mend daily; whilst the docked ones grow every hour more and more out of condition."

—Henry Herbert, 10th EARL OF PEMBROKE. (3 July 1734 – 26 January 1794) In 1761 he wrote the British Army's manual on riding, Military Equitation: or A Method of Breaking Horses, and Teaching Soldiers to Ride - this had already reached a 4th edition by 1793, and his methods were adopted throughout the British cavalry.

CHAPTER XX

On the hunting horse

Although hunting is considered only an amusement, the exercise merits attention, since it is preferred by kings and princes, above all others. This preference is without a doubt founded upon the affinity between the chase and war; in each, there is an object to attain, fatigue to be endured, dangers to avoid, and stratagems[20] to practice. It is not then surprising that and exercise which bears such a relation to the heroic sentiments inseparable from great princes, should fix the fashion of their pleasures. This is not the place to examine all the different modes of hunting; but the life of a beloved sovereign is so precious to his subjects, that it becomes our particular province to employ every means in its preservation. We have already said, that the chase has its dangers in common with war; but the greatest part of these dangers arises from ill-chosen and ill-trained horses for which reason we have carefully endeavored to find out the means of acquiring the knowledge of a good hunter, and the readiest and surest mode of dressing [training] him to the exercise.

Many people think the method followed to dress [train] horses in the school is contrary to that which ought to be followed for hunters and troop horses. This opinion, though badly founded, is the cause of neglecting true principles. There is no guide left but the bad example of those who gave rise to this opinion, and persevere in the erroneous practice. The result acquired is only a kind of firmness without grace; the execution is forced and without [a principled] foundation. How can anyone, who possesses even a small degree of judgment, pretend to say, that a rider, capable of putting into practice the principles of good schooling, by which he is able to discern the nature of this horse and his horse to a [specific] air, does not possess the art of suppling a horse designed for war, and of making him obedient? Or that he cannot extend a horse designed for the chase and give him wind? Aren't these the first principles of the art of riding?

The choice of a good hunter is very difficult to make; besides the exterior qualities of other horses, he ought to have particularly good lungs, lightness and to be sure-footed. These qualities ought to be natural to the hunting horse, for at best, art can only perfect them.

---

20   A plan, scheme, or trick for outwitting or deceiving an enemy.

A hunter ought not to be thick shouldered, nor very short in his body; because such horses are commonly short-winded, and do not possess the speed necessary for a good hunter. He ought to be rather long in the body, have his neck raised, his shoulders free and flat, his legs large and nervous, but not long jointed; he ought to be naturally swift, sensible to the spur, and in a light *appui* [contact].

Monsieur de la Broue says, that:
"Horses unfit for the chase are those which natural timidity prevents from going fast for fear of running the hazards of the hunt, those which are dissident of their strength from some natural or accidental defects, those which are by nature heavy and sluggish, and those which are blemished, those which like better to make leaps than to ration their strength over the duration of the course, and lastly those which retain their powers from malice and cowardice."

Even though all these different types of horses may be actually trained for the chase [hunt], they cannot acquire the qualities of good hunters, which are to gallop light, sure-footed, and long-winded. These qualities are only to be found where there is a natural flexibility in the limbs, which is perfected by the trot, freedom in the shoulders, and a light *appui* [contact] in the mouth, that one confirms in the gallop with sufficient wind and courage augmented by exercise.

The trot, which is the first gait in which to supple all kinds of horses, ought to be long and extended, rather than elevated so that the horse may learn to throw out his forearms and shoulders. The bridoon is excellent to give the horse this first suppleness. With this instrument, which we have described before, a horse may be easily bent, without being constrained too much. He may be taught to turn readily and freely in both directions, without offending the bars of his mouth and the place where the curb [will later be used], nor disturbing the mouth. The bridoon can help make the horse as flexible as his strengths and his disposition allow him to become. He must be trotted in both directions, without any regard to terrain, but to constantly vary the order of the lessons; sometimes to the right, sometimes to the left, on the circle; and sometimes on a straight line, with greater then less length [of stride] depending on his inclination, either to retain [hold back] or abandon himself [be too free.]

He must be kept to the trot until he obeys the slightest motion of the hand and legs, and has learned to turn with ease, readily, and freely, [equally] in both directions. When he arrives at this point, he should be fitted with a bit suited to his mouth; after which is given the lesson of the shoulder-in, not only to supple his sides and to form his mouth, but essentially to teach him to move with his inside hind leg under his belly [center of gravity.] This is a skill that is absolutely necessary for a hunter, so that he can gallop more smoothly, more conveniently and more gracefully[21].

In putting him to the shoulder-in, he must be kept a little together [somewhat collected,] but not in a posture as short as if he were trained in the *manège*; on the contrary, he must be more extended, to give him greater facility to throw out his legs and shoulders. However, he must not be laid out so much as to acquire the fault of bearing upon the hand; for this he must be corrected by halts, half-halts, and reining-back.

After the lesson of the trot has been perfected by the incorporation of the shoulder-in, the halts, the half-halts and the rein-back, the horse must be cantered to augment the lightness of his shoulders, to settle and soften the appui [contact] of the mouth, and confirm him in the hunting gallop.

This freedom of the shoulders, one of the most essential properties of a hunter, is easily acquired after the horse has been regulated by the lessons in the trot and the rider knows how to extend the horse's shoulders and make him throw out his legs. The motion of the canter should neither become too high nor too close to the ground. The first error, [cantering too high in the shoulder and forearms] is called swimming in the canter [*nager en gallopant*], and would not have the capacity to extend [lengthen stride.] The second error [cantering too low to the ground], would cause the horse to stumble at every little raised section of ground or stone he should meet with due to "shaving too close to the carpet" [*en rasant de trop près le tapis*] moving too near to the ground.

It must be agreed that nature seems to have formed some horses on purpose, and has given them this free extended movement of the shoulders, which constitutes the true merit of a hunter. The English horses, above all horses of Europe, have this quality, and consequently are seen to perform their course with incredible swiftness. At their races held at Newmarket [a market town in the county of Suffolk, England], the horse that wins the prize must run four English miles, which is about two short French leagues in eight minutes, sometimes less. Their hunters often run a whole day without being unbridled, and are always close to their hounds in their fox chase, and leap over all hedges and ditches, which are numerous in a country so much cut and enclosed as England.

---

21 Note de la Gueriniere's recommendation on the direct benefits of the shoulder-in in the trot to improve the canter and the gallop.-Editor's note.

I am persuaded that if the English horses were to be suppled by the rules of this art, they would gallop with greater ease [more sure-footed], and more comfortably to their rider. Their legs wouldn't be ruined as soon as is often the case; for after two or three years of service, their legs tremble under them. The reason of this weakness, which does not appear to be natural, but more likely accidental, comes without a doubt from galloping the horses too young, without having been previously suppled at the trot, and from the fact that they are galloped always with the snaffle, whereas it should only be used in the beginning to supple them. This instrument is not designed to support the front end, nor to give the horse support. Sometimes a horse has no relief in his gallop; and the weight of the rider, combined with that of his own shoulders, neck and head, fatigues the nerves, tendons and ligaments of the legs, by which they are soon ruined, and the defect of stumbling or flinching is produced. For this reason, the old masters invented the curb bit, to support the action of the horse in all his paces, particularly his gallop; in which as he is more extended, and is more prone to take on false [*fausse*: distorted or skewed] positions.

When a horse, intended for a hunter, is first galloped, he must not be galloped very much extended; because, as he does not yet have the habit of galloping freely, he will bear upon the hand; neither must his gallop be too short; for that would impede from using himself as he should. But he must be galloped united; without restraining him, nor chasing him forward too much; and just as if he galloped by himself, of his own accord, without a rider. It is the light hand, accompanied by frequent descents of the hand [*descents de main*] that gives the gallop the qualities that we described. The descent of the hand, which is an excellent aid in every air, seems to have been invented expressly for hunters, to teach them to gallop without a bridle [curb bit], and without obliging the rider to support them at all. This lesson of the canter must be performed on a large circle and on the smaller one as was done in the trot, and sometimes on the straight line [first to one direction, then to the other.] The intervals should not be too long at first, for that would harass and fatigue the horse, instead of strengthening his wind and forming his gallop. One should cease the gallop and return to the walk relatively often, to give him time to get his breath. As soon as he is refreshed, put him to the gallop again. This method of changing alternately from the gallop to the walk without stopping entirely, gradually builds stamina in the horse to the extent that his strength allows. The rider must be the judge of the length of the course of the gallop; when he perceives the horse out of breath, he ought to put him to the walk. Gradually the rider should shorten the duration of the walk period, when he finds the horse able to continue longer in the gallop. Another focus of consequence deserving note is that at the end of every gallop [or canter], the horse should pass at once to the walk, without making a single step in the trot, between the two paces [between canter and walk]; because it is very troublesome to the rider; and also, that the horse set off from the walk to the gallop, [without any trot steps] it has to be done at once.

When the horse begins to develop lung capacity [wind,] and can canter for longer periods, without blowing or sweating excessively, then he may be asked to extend the canter, which is called the hunting gallop [*galop de chasse*]. Do this without subjecting to the posture of the head restricted to the observance of the rule of keeping the horse's face perpendicular to the ground, [form the fore-head to the nose], as in the *manège*; instead, the head should be left a little more at liberty, so that he may open his nostrils wider and breathe more freely. Still, he must not be allowed to carry his nose high in the wind. Galloping with his head high and misplaced makes him more liable to fall than if the horse can see the ground on which he is about to put down his feet.

There is a very excellent lesson that I have seen put in practice by able masters, to train horses for the hunt. It is to gallop in a large circle to the left, and to keep the horse bent slightly to the right, united with the right lead. This method of turning to the left, though the horse gallops on the right lead, teaches him not to become disunited when it is necessary to reverse his shoulder, that is to turn short to the left, which would often happen if he were not formed to this motion, and occasion an irregularity, that would greatly incommode[22] the rider, and disorder his seat. The old masters had a method of which I greatly approve for galloping their horses of war and for the hunt; it was to gallop the horse on a serpentine line; instead of a whole circle, they continually made sections of circles, turning the shoulders every moment without changing lead, describing a path that is roughly the same as that of a snake or an eel while crawling. Nothing else confirms a horse on his feet nor assures him on his legs better than this exercise. It is easily practiced once the horse has been properly prepared by cantering on a circle to the left, on the united right lead [and vice versa.]

As we said in the preceding chapter, a horse trained for the hunt or for war must not be confined to the grove of the *manège* only. He must be exercised in the open country, so he can become accustomed to all kinds of objects, and so that he can learn to gallop sure-footedly on all kinds of terrain such as tilled fields, soft ground, meadows, downhill inclines, climb mountains, valleys, woods, etc.

---

22   To inconvenience or discomfort; disturb; trouble.

We will not repeat here that it is necessary to accustom the horse to stand fire, which is an essential for a courier or runner [messenger]; but another quality particularly important for a hunting horse is to leap over hedges and ditches so that he may not be stopped by such obstacles.

Monsieur de la Broue gives us a lesson on this subject, which I believe is both practical and good. It is to lay a hurdle three or four feet wide, and ten or twelve long. Lay it flat upon the ground at first and make a horse jump over it in the walk, the trot, and the gallop. If he puts his feet upon it, chastise him with the birch switch and with the spurs. After this, the hurdle is to be raised about a foot from the ground, so that he learns to leap over it freely, it is to be raised higher and higher, till it gets to the proper height [3-4 feet], and then it is to be garnished with branches and leaves. This method, which he says he has been often practiced safely, teaches a horse to extend himself to leap over hedges and ditches; but this lesson, which is necessary for both the war horse and the hunting horse, ought to be taught, only after the horse has learned to be obedient to turn in both directions, moves off and stops well, has had his head well-placed [*placée*], and his mouth assured with a proper contact.

There is another type of horse for hunting that is called, *Chevaux arquebus* [Named after the type of gun their rider's carried, the harquebus, a small caliber long gun dating from 1400. Named from Middle Dutch *hākebusse:* hook + box, after the shape of the butt]. These were usually small horses that were trained for hunting with guns. These horses should have the same qualities as the other hunting horses [*coureurs*] but they should be perfectly inured to the sound of gunfire and to the sounds of game birds flushing and taking off. They are usually trained to stop on the voice command: "*Hou;*" but the more subtle and best trained horses learn to stop short even from the gallop without stirring at the moment the rider drops the reins onto the neck. A well-trained *arquebus* horse is much sought after, but of paramount importance in the training is great *patience*, rather than science (which is still essential.) We won't go into greater detail, since what we have described seems sufficient.

CHAPTER XXI

On Carriage Horses

In former ages, magnificent *equipages*[23] were only used for the celebration of triumphs, without attention to their commodiousness; but modern luxury, with incredible progress, has given rise to the construction of many and various descriptions of carriages and the most common of those on the present day, infinitely surpass those ancient cars.

The most essential improvement arises from the carriages being suspended upon the axil by delicate springs, which render the motion almost imperceptible; and the lightness of the workmanship considerably diminishes the labor of the horses.

When no improvement could be make in the construction of the carriage, more attention was paid to decoration, which has been so successful that nothing is more capable of announcing rank and dignity than the magnificence of an equipage, if the horses were better chosen and dressed for harness. Negligence in this point was pardonable in other times, because the labor required dragging heavy, ill-shaped machines necessarily precluded graceful action. At present there is nothing to prevent our producing that elegant superb appearance seldom though sometimes seen.

Germany took the lead on the continent of Europe, and the example was followed by several French noblemen. It is however much to be desired that the custom should become general, not only for appearance, but to prevent those accidents, which too often happen, in putting to a carriage horses that have neither been suppled, nor had their mouths made.

Enough is in general supposed to be done to prevent danger, by harnessing new horses, and putting them to the carriage, three or four times before they are brought into use; yet we have almost daily examples, to convince us, this precipitate mode is extremely inadequate to preclude danger, or prevent the horses from trotting ungracefully, irregularly, upon their shoulders, with the head down, the croup high, or forcing the hand; faults the more remarkable, in proportion to the magnificence of the carriages.

Let us now describe the qualities necessary for carriage horses, and the means of dressing them.

23   A carriage drawn by horses and attended by servants.

A coach horse ought to have his head well placed, his neck raised, and to trot straight and united in the traces; he should be from fifteen to sixteen hands high, well turned, and high before, even though his back be rather low, which would be a defect in a saddle horse; he should be full bodied, yet his shoulders ought not to be loaded, nor his breast too large, though these qualities would be proper in wagon horses, because they would pull better in the traces.

Coach horses should have flat supple shoulders, in order to trot freely and gracefully; they should be neither long nor short, but of a middling length; for those which are very short, generally ever-reach, and those which are very long, press upon the bit, for want of strength, in the reins, to keep them up; they ought to have clean, well-proportioned limbs, and a good deal of bone, but above all good feet. Great attention should be paid to the hocks, because coach horses are more liable to have defects in them than lighter horses; fetlocks that bend too much hinder coach horses from reining back, and holding back as they go downhill.

A well-chosen coach horse, possessing the qualities above mentioned, certainly deserves the pains necessary to give him the first principles of a dressed horse, suppleness and obedience. With these perfections, he will trot with more grace, and last longer. First trot him on the longe, afterwards mount him, and put him to shoulder-in; to bend him, give him a fine posture, and form his mouth: he ought also to be taught to pass his legs, by the croup to the wall, that he may make his turnings with more ease; for every time a coach horse turns, he describes on two tracks, a circular line with his haunches and shoulders, with is a kind of demi-volte, and to perform this, he ought to know how to pass his legs freely, both before and behind, otherwise he would strike them against each other, strain his haunches, or turn awkwardly; he ought to be taught to piaffe perfectly well in the pillars, after he has been suppled in the trot; for nothing gives a coach horse a finer air, than the piaffe in the pillars. The pillars make him stand in awe of the whip, and obedient to the slightest motions of that aid.

Another thing, which is however seldom seen, is that a coach horse ought to be bent to the hand to which he is to go, the off horse to the right, and the near horse to the left; this posture makes him appear more graceful, enables him to see his road, keeps his croup upon the line of the shoulders, and makes him trot firm and united. Those which do not trot in this posture put their heads down towards the pole, which throws the croup out against the traces, or else they stretch out their noses and pull upon the hand which is more dangerous, because they have it in their power to force the coachman's hand, which is vulgarly called taking the bit in their teeth, by which those in the carriage, and people on foot, are alike exposed to the danger of their lives. It is very common to see one horse in a coach lower his nose and the other horse raise it, which is both disagreeable and discordant, and could not happen if they had been properly broke. If anyone should be surprised that I recommend the same principles for coach horses as for those of the *manège*, I only desire that he look at the *equipage* of those gentlemen who are attentive to their horses, and he will instantly perceive the difference between horses that are dressed, and those that are not. I do not say that a coach horse should be confirmed in obedience to the hand and heel, like a *manèged* horse, but only that he be unstiffened, and have his mouth made, be taught to piaffe, respect the whip, and obey its slightest motion; nor do I recommend these rules for all coach horses, but only for such as from figure and price are worthy of this attention; clumsy, ill-made horses, may be left to the care of the coachman.

CHAPTER XXII

On tournaments, jousts, carousels, and contests

In all periods of history, cohorts of men have been trained in skill to prepare them for war, even today.

The Romans had racing, wrestling, man to man combat, freehand and with various weaponry, combats with beasts and tricks on horseback which would have made them more agile once they joined the army.

Foot racing gave them speed.

Wrestling gave them strength.

Man to man combat taught them to fight and nurtured the killer spirit.

The combat between man and beast despite improving fighting skills and foresight, was banned due to its barbarousness by the Emperor Constantine.

Circus tricks on horseback improved competence in chariot driving, so that the driver could control up to as many as eight horses via the reins without losing speed or colliding.

Military exercises schooled warriors for battle. They made princes and the nobility adept at horsemanship. Thus tournaments, jousts, carousels and races became a kind of school for battle for the nobility and those who were identified as excellent natural horsemen who could be trained as cavalry officers.

FIRST ARTICLE

On Tournaments

History books credit Emperor Commenus of Constantinople with the invention of tournaments. They began as horse races that incorporated turns (*tournois*). Then came sticks thrown at the opponents warded off by shields, first documented in Troy, then Rome, then by the Turks, the Persians and through the Orient.

The Moors ornamented their arms and armor with Arabic writing and numerals. They decorated their devices and armor with symbolic colors: black being sadness, green being hope, white representing purity, red being cruelty. By this diversity of fanfare, their tournaments became spectacles and at the conclusion, a ladies' ball was thrown and the ladies administered the prizes.

Other nations added to these customs. Goths and Germans added winged dragons, harpies, lions to their cloaks and a feather on the top of their helmets, called a crest.

The French embellished their arms and armor with their coats of arms, to identify the knight. Eventually, these became a mark of nobility and ultimately evolved the family crests of the great houses of Europe.

Emperor Heinrich I, also named 'The fowler,' promoted these tournaments for sport and entertainment to the nobility in the tenth century. They were stopped at the end of the fifteen century because the nobility became weak and soft.

SECOND ARTICLE

On Jousts

Jousts were races using lances. These were at close range, thus the Latin name *juxta pugnare*. Two knights armed with lances galloped toward each other along a barrier dividing them and upon meeting at the center, struck each other. The point was to unseat and throw the other rider to the ground, sometimes with his mount.

Especially popular in France, princes and nobility competed with competent gentlemen without consideration of rank, until Henri II abolished jousts and replaced them with the Head and Ring Contests of the Carousels.

THIRD ARTICLE

On Carousels

Military festivals called carousels were performed by troops of riders divided into teams or quadrilles. Prizes were awarded for the winners of each battle exercise.

These military festivals showcased chariots, war machines, decorations, devices and equestrian ballets. The festivities were intended to impress the princes and other nobility.

A true carousel included:
1. The colonel and his *aides de camp*.
2. The quadrille riders.
3. Cartels, names, dress, devices, arms, engines of war, pages, thralls, foot valets, attendants, horses and their ornaments.
4. The recitations of the speakers.
5. The designers of the engines of war.
6. The musicians.
7. The races.
8. The prizes.

The colonel organizes the march, files out the quadrille, leads competitors out onto the track and into the tilt rings. He is the master of ceremonies.

The *aides de camp* serve the colonel and carry out his orders.

The smallest number of riders in a quadrille is usually four; the largest is twelve (not including the leader.) They should be of an even number so that the number of members is equal in the contests.

The smallest number of quadrille competitions is four and can be up to twelve.

The two types of quadrilles are those of the Challengers and those of the Assault.

The challengers open the carousel and make the first challenges through cartels which the heroes announce. They are called challengers because they challenge any who approach to engage at arms. They are the first quadrille.

The cartel is named for the leader of the quadrille. The cartels include five elements:
1. The name and title of the members challenged.
2. The subject event, the Challengers challenged.
3. Some personal statements about them to make it more interesting.
4. The place and manor of the combat.
5. The name of the Challengers who send the challenge or Cartel members, names' taken from history or legend.

These cartels may be in prose or verse, and since the aim of these challenges is to acquire glory and to gain notoriety, they tend to be rife with boastfulness (*rodomontade*). Princes are excused from these challenges so that the cartels may be given to others.

Since the subject matter of carousels is historic, from fables and emblematic, the lieutenants and assailants take on names that fit with the topic they represent: for example, if Romans are being portrayed, they take on names like Julius Caesar, Augustus, etc.

One can also take on the names from novels such as *Chevaliers du Lys, du Soleil, du Rose* etc. [Knights of Lys, the Sun, the Rose etc..] Sometimes the names are pure invention like *Forimonde, Lisandre*, etc.

The names should speak to the 'currency' of the riders, and the Quadrille should also take on the name. Their costumes, the livery, their weapons, their machines, their slaves, their cartels should be all be uniform.

The Pages are usually mounted; they carry the lances and the equipment.

The foot valets and attendants lead the horses by hand and look after the machines of war. They may be disguised as Turks, Moors, slaves, heathens, Armenians, monkeys, bears, according to the theme and the desire of the leader of the Quadrille.

The recitations, the music and the majority of the machines of war that serve to enhance the pomp of the Carousel, are the inventions of the Italians, who always achieve the greatest refinement and who have excelled in this genre.

The people who recite, and operate the machines are as actors in the theatre, who represent diverse things according to the theme. Sometimes, they recite allegorical prose honoring those for whom these festivals are held.

The musicians give vocal and instrumental concerts and the harmonies used in these festivals are of two types: the first is military, so to speak, fierce and war-like, the other is soft and agreeable. The first type is played at the beginning of each quadrille and serves to animate the riders, and to announce their arrival, their entrance into the ring, called *comparse*[24], and during their races. The second type is played during recitations, use of the machines and for general pomp and processionals

For martial music, the trumpets, drums, tympanis, oboes, and fifes, are used.

For the sweeter music the violins, flutes, oboes, bagpipes etc. are used. These instruments also accompany the dances, the equestrian ballet as we will explain in the article called "On the *foule*."

ARTICLE IV

On the contests

All of the preceding refers to the processional and organizational aspects of the carousel. The principal parts of the carousel are the races for which prizes are awarded and in which the riders may display their equestrian prowess.

The most considerable tournaments that were practiced in the past consisted of breaking lances against the one another; a tilting at the Quintaine[25], a sword fighting on horseback, sword in hand, a stag's head and ring contests; and the *foule* [crowd].

We have already described that during the jousts, lances would be broken. With the invention of firearms the practice of jousting in combat was abandoned, and the contest also fell from favor because it was very dangerous.

Lances were also broken when used on the Quintaine (target); this was a very ancient challenge game named after its inventor,

---

24   From the Italian, *comparsa*: extra, walk-on, spear-bearer, supernumerary.- Editor's note.
25   A post or target set up for tilting [to aim or thrust (a lance) in a joust] exercises for mounted knights or foot soldiers or the exercise of tilting at such a target.

Quintus [means fifth born son]. A trunk of tree or a pillar was also used as targets for lances, in order to train for striking the opponent with considerable force. Later this game was named *faquin* [scoundrel], because a fully armored mannequin was used as the target. However the most common way was a figure made of wood shaped like a man mounted on a pivot so that it was mobile. This target was also designed so that it would remain still when struck directly on the forehead, between the eyes or directly on the nose (these were the best strikes.) When the mannequin was struck anywhere else on the body, it would spin so quickly that if the knight was not skilled enough to evade it, the mannequin would strike the knight rudely on the back with a wooden sword attached to its hand as it spun around.

In the sword fight on horseback, the riders started out between the tilting ring and the place where the princes sat. Separated by forty paces, two riders faced each other, sword in hand and awaited the sound of the trumpet. Upon hearing the trumpets they lowered the bridle hand [left] and raised the sword and departed with great speed towards each other. Upon meeting, they struck each other with the flat side of the great sword and each turned slightly to the left. Once reaching the spot from which their adversary had set out, the performed a half-volte and repeated the charge and strike as many as three times. After the third strike, instead of going back to the point of origin and making another half-volte, the opponents rode on a volte, facing each other, continuously striking each other with the Great sword with great verve until they had each completed three *voltes*, at which point they returned to their respective points of origin pretending to do another half-volte, when another set of riding opponents would replace them and compete doing the same sequence.

The Constable of Montmorenci was very famous for this exercise and one wishes it were still more commonly in use, because it was a very important maneuver of war, teaching how to handle the sword and the pistol. And it was not dangerous because the blows with the sword could be delivered above the opponent's head and even the shots from the pistol could be fired up into the air.

Of all the contests which were part of the ancient tournaments and carousels, the only two that remain in use in the modern [18th century] academies are those of the head and the ring. They are the subject of the next two articles.

ARTICLE V

On the head contest

The Germans practiced this exercise before the French: the wars with the Turks gave occasion to do so. They practiced by charging at figures of heads of Turks and of Moors against which they threw 'darts' [*le dard:* a short javelin] and fire the pistols, and struck others with the point of swords. All of this was to practice recouping the heads of their fallen [and beheaded] comrades in order to prevent the Turkish soldiers from carrying of the heads for which they would be able to claim bounty from their superior officers.

The lance, the 'dart,' the sword and the pistol were used in the head contest.

The lance is composed of the spearhead, the shaft, the hand and the wings. It is about six feet long.

The 'dart' is a shaft of hardwood about three feet long, pointed at one end. Imbedded in the wood are small iron buttons marking the place to hold it [in the middle] so that it will remain in balance in the rider's hand.

In a well-organized contest, there are usually four heads made of cardboard. The first, for the lance, is mounted on a metal stand attached to the wall or to a pillar in the *manège*. The stand is mobile and turns on two small axles; it should be about two feet long and be about eight feet off the ground.

The second head is the head of Medusa, flat and about one foot in diameter, (more or less) attached to a sort of board a little larger than the first. It is attached to a wooden stand which should put the height of the head at about five feet above the ground, or it can also be mounted on the fence of the *manège* [at the same height.]

The third head is that of a Moor, placed like that of Medusa on top of a wooden stand at the same height or on the fence of the *manège*.

The fourth head is for the sword and should be on the ground on a small mound [of dirt] about two and a half feet from the edge of the *manège*.

The four heads should be placed along the long side of the *manège* which should (as we have said before) be a rectangle 120 feet long by 36 feet wide. With these dimensions, the first head (for the lance) should be placed about two thirds of the way down the wall, or 80 feet from the corner of the *manège*, where one will make the first volte.

The second head (of Medusa) should be placed 5 feet from the wall on the same side as the [first] head for the lance and on the half arena line [sixty feet from each corner]. It should be mounted on the wooden stand if the *manège* is enclosed with walls; but if there are no walls, it can be mounted on the fence at the half way point in the middle of the long side. The head of the Moor should be placed opposite it, on the other long side,

The fourth head (intended for the sword), is placed on the ground on the same long side as that of the Moor, about two and a half feet from the wall and forty feet from the corner where one finishes the course.

When one uses the pistol, one attaches a cardboard figure to the wall at the height of head of a man on horseback. Some riders chose to shoot with the pistol at the Moor's head rather than using the 'dart' since the pistol is more useful for this type of target [killing, rather than recouping.]

One thing that is difficult in the contest of the heads is to raise the lance well and with grace. In order to accomplish this, begin three horse's lengths from the corner where one starts with a half-volte, then take some time with the horse standing still in one place; the lance in the right hand and posed on the middle of the [rider's] thigh. This is called 'holding off' (*la tenir en arrêt.*) The point of the lance is held slight above and in front of the horse's right ear.

Before departing to the collected canter, which should be united and *rassemblé* [put together], one should begin by lifting the arm with the lance, with the index finger extended and pointing along the length of the lance toward the point, lifting the elbow to the height of the rider's shoulder, and from the elbow to the wrist the arm is held straight in front, so as to form a right angle from wrist to elbow and from elbow to shoulder. If the hand of the lance were level with and close to the rider's head, the lance would hit the rider in the face, and if the lance hand and arm of the rider are too high or too low, the form would lack grace.

The lance is also placed in this manner in the half-*volte*. Therefore one must adhere to the necessary movements to carry the lance so that it is poised for the attack of the head. There are four principle movements. The first is to lower the index finger and the wrist a little and also raise the elbow without changing the exact position of the point of the lance. The second is to lower the arm imperceptibly to the side of the body close to the [rider's] hip. The third is to open the wrist to the outside and raise the lance arm to the side of the body without bringing the lance forward or backward and extending the arm until it is above and to the side of the [rider's] head. The fourth is to turn the fingernails toward one's head and imperceptibly [slowly] lower the lance back to the first position, i.e. with the elbow at the height of the shoulder.

The lance contest is divided into three parts. In the first, one

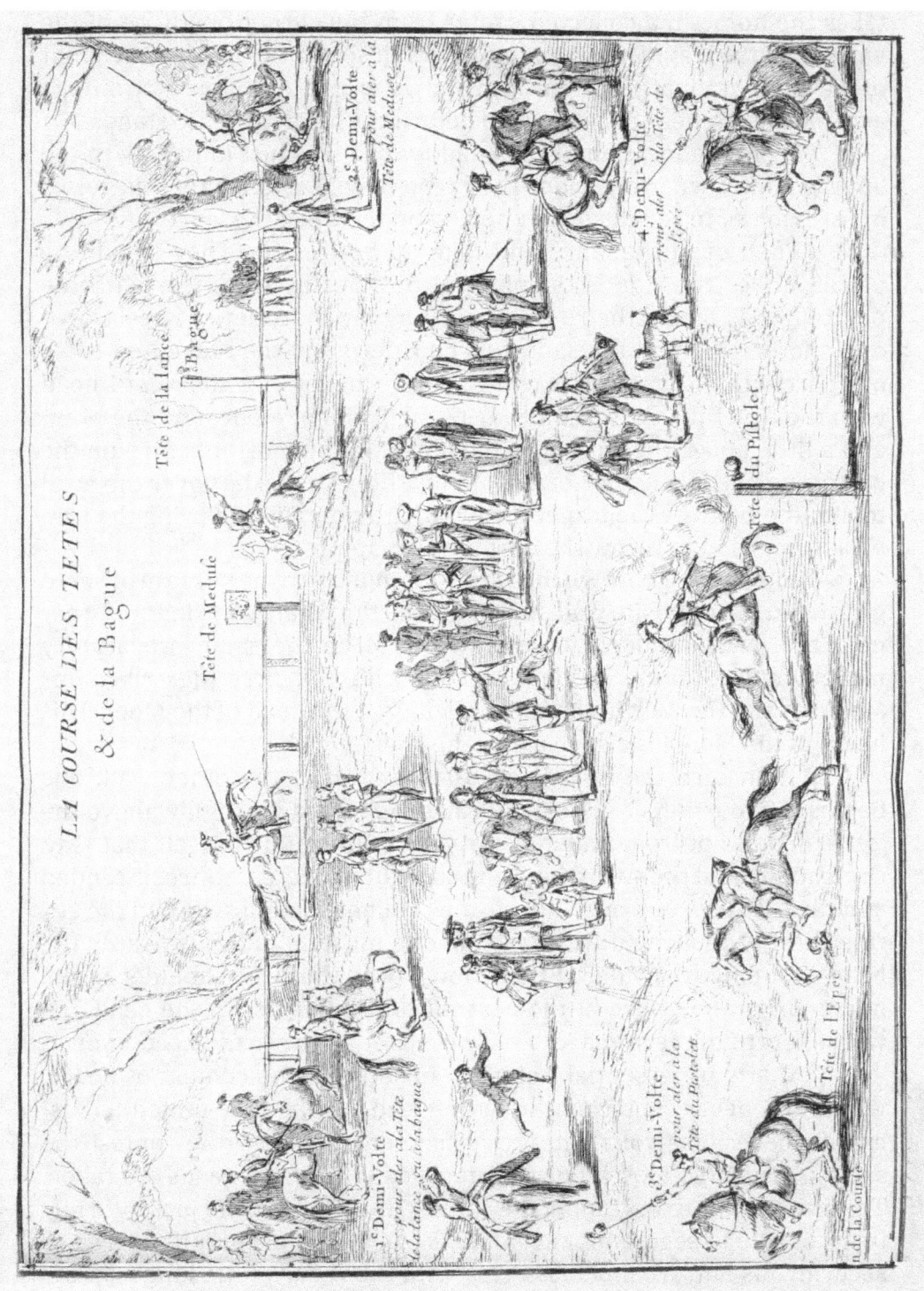

The head and ring contest

takes the horse in a collected canter from the corner one third of the way down the wall. Then proceeding at full speed, one lowers the point of the lance gradually on approach and delivers a sharp thrust from the arm [at the moment of contact] to detach the head from the stand.

From the location of the head [which was just impaled], to the approaching corner one rides the horse in collected canter and raises his arm for all to see the head impaled on the tip of the lance.

Then drop the lance and take up both darts. They should be placed under the rider's thighs, kept in place by his knees with the pointed ends facing the rump in such a way that they intersect over one another [behind the saddle.] The rider must then take and carry one dart with the free arm extended a little higher than the rider's head with the tip of the dart to the side of the [rider's] elbow and the blunt end a little above the left ear of the horse. In this position, turn on the half arena line facing the head of Medusa. Rotate the dart over the head to aim the point at the target throw it. The rider should bring the arm back somewhat to throw the dart with greater force.

After having thrown the 'dart,' one must turn the horse in order to go toward the opposite wall, and make the third half-volte in the corner near the head intended for the sword. Make the same preparatory movements with the second dart as with the first [described for Medusa] and throw it in the same manner at the head of the Moor. This head [of the Moor] is also used for the short pistol.

Then turn the horse and upon arrival at the other wall, one begins the fourth half-volte and draws the sword gracefully above the left arm and not from under it, for you could maim yourself that way. One should hold the sword high and straight with the free arm extended and raise it above the head 'to stir the brilliant shining sword in the air.' One third of the way down the wall, one must go full tilt towards the head, stooping [the rider's] body down onto the right shoulder of the horse. Bring the sword at the next third into the face of the head and with a fourth of the arena left, raise it up for all to see the head upon it.

There are essential points to observe in the contest of heads, which are: never canter on the wrong lead, nor in a dis-united [cross] canter; never lose your hat, if that happens, you lose the contest the same is true if you lose your stirrup, even if all of the heads are taken. This is why, before beginning the contest, the rider should just sit firmly in his saddle to secure his seat and his placement in stirrups as well as securing his hat. We must also ride with the reins a little longer in the contest than in the closed *manège* so that the horse has the freedom to extend the gaits without the rider giving up the contact entirely so that the rider and the horse are more assured in the race.

ARTICLE VI

The Ring Contest

This contest was not done in antiquity; it was introduced out of gallantry when ladies began judging the exercises. Here the targets which were previously military targets, were changed to rings which were to be carried off with the point of the lance to claim the prize.

The ring should be placed two thirds of the way down the course at the height of the mounted rider's forehead above the right ear of the horse.

The *potence* is a round wooden stick about two feet long at the end of which the ring is suspended. The *potence* is attached to another piece of wood called a canon. This *potence* should be raised seven to eight inches above the ring so that it will not be collided with during the contest. This would cause serious injury to the rider, and has happened more than once.

The raising of the lance is done in the same way as was described earlier in the description of the head contest. The only difference is that in the ring contest, one does not give a quick thrust as was the case with the contest of the heads.

Once again, we must pay attention not to lower the tip of the lance until one is one third of the way down the length of the course where the horse is taken into the full gallop [from the collected canter.] Take care to keep the [rider's] head and shoulders still, holding the elbow high so that the shaft of the lance does touches neither the arms nor the body and the only support for the lance is from the rider's hand. It is also important that the lance should not cross beyond the left ear of the horse. On the contrary, it should be carried above the right ear of the horse because otherwise the wind would shake it out of the position of the direction of the line of travel [aimed at the ring.] The goal or the object of the contest should be to aim at the top of the ring near the canon. Therefore, take care not to lower the tip of the lance too quickly.

After having passed the ring, one should again take up the collected canter and raise, little by little, the point of the lance and at the end of the run raise the lance in the same way as in the beginning without looking back to see if the ring was taken, (as some riders do) when they are finished. One must neither pet the horse nor lean back at the end of the course. These actions are unseemly in the lance in-hand contest.

In the terminology of the ring contest, it is called "making an attack" or "striking a blow" [*faire un atteinte*] when the lance touches the top edge of the ring without taking it, and it is called "making it inside" or "striking home" [*faire un dedans*] when the ring is taken and successfully carried off.

Sometimes, one takes the ring by the navel, which is a hole where the ring is attached. This is worthless unless the rider states in advance, that he plans on taking the ring this way.

With regard to the prize, for the ring contest as for the contest of the heads, each rider makes three runs at the course.

He who takes the most rings wins the contest of the rings. If there is a tie, or if no rings are taken, the contest must be started over.

In the Carousel, the judges are chosen from the older riders, who made themselves famous in the exercises.

There used to be many prizes; for example the Grand Prize, which was given to the one who had taken the highest number of rings or the one who had won the most heads, or the one who had the most blows to the quintaine. There was a prize for the course of the ladies, a prize for the best device, and for the one who ran the course with the most grace.

ARTICLE VII.

The Foule Contest

The name *foule* in the carousel comes from an Italian phrase, *far la Fola,* where at the same time several riders handle a given number of horses in different figures.

This performance is a type of horse ballet done to the accompaniment of several musical instruments: it was invented by the Italians, who ornamented their carousels with an infinite number of gallant inventions which made the spectacle both surprising and enjoyable.

The horses must be well-trained and well-adjusted, and the riders must be experienced and skilled in order to execute this type of performance. It takes great skill to maintain the distances between the horses, the shape of the figures and to maintain the regularity of the airs and the cadence.

To give an accurate idea of all of the *foules* that one might invent, we give an example.

Along each of the long walls or barriers of the *manège* four riders are lined up about ten or twelve feet apart (more or less, according to the size of the *manège*), to ensure that [later] the riders on one side will be able to turn inward (in unison) to the right and the riders on the opposite wall will be able to turn inward to the left (in unison) so as to face each other. Meanwhile, three more riders are located on the centerline. These eleven riders should form three lines and they should have the head of their horse facing one of the end walls of the *manège*.

The eight riders on the long walls, (four on each side) make half-voltes, changes of hand continuously, each on his own (small) area of the *manège*; as for the three on the centerline, the middle one makes pirouettes and the other two ride voltes, one to the right and the other the left.

The riders should all begin together at the signal of the one who is conducting the carousel and halt at the end of the display in the same way (together in unison) or they could Courbette or perform whatever air each of the horses has been trained to do.

All of the exercises which we have described and explained in this chapter were invented to give an agreeable image and to be instructive for the war horse and to encourage emulation among the nobility. The exercises were used in Italy around the end of the 16th century. Rome and Naples were the homes of the most celebrated academies to which members of other nations came to perfect their skills and practice these exercises which formerly were the diversions of princes and nobility. They sought to distinguish themselves and render themselves capable to serve their ruler with honor and to acquire the virtues and talents that were inseparable with those in the profession of arms.

The End of Part II

Appendix from Part I

CHAPTER VI

On the Bridle

The very first bridles that were used were nothing but a simple piece of wood or iron rounded to fit the shape of the horse's mouth. They did not have branches or shanks and were fitted with two long cords attached on either side of the horse's mouth. Later, shanks were added to the place where previously, the ropes were attached, and a type of rein was now attached to the bottom of the shanks on each side. But it was discovered that this instrument had insufficient effect, and the curb chain was thus invented so that the bridle worked better by acting on the bars of the mouth and likewise the chain on the groove of the chin. The help of the reins acting on the branches produces a leverage effect and activates the bit and the curb chain with practical implementation, simultaneously.

The majority of the riders in the past, believed that all of the obedience that one could ask of the horse was dependent on the way in which the bridle was designed. The bridles were made of a multitude of pieces both fixed and moving, with various effects caused by rude bits and curb chains that were too short, obligating the horse to strain at the rider's hand, to the point of running off and going at the bit without stopping; this type of grand subjection produced despair in the horses instead of obedience.

At the end of the sixteenth century, [Giovanni Battista] Pignatelli, famous riding master, greatly reputed at the school of Naples [southern Italy including Sicily], did not spend much time in this error. Instead, he invented a kind of bit composed of three moving pieces which resembled a yoke which was infinitely softer than those that had been in use up to that point. Convinced by proper experience, he believed that the bridle should only serve to warn the horse of the rider's will rather than to force the horse. He said that if bridles themselves had the ability to miraculously form the mouth of a horse, and to render him obedient, then rider and horse would be fully trained upon leaving the bit-maker's shop [*epronnier*].

Therefore, we will only speak further about the bridles which do not offend horses' mouths. The opinion of most good riding masters confirmed by experience, proves to us that the most simple and the most soft bits, that conserve the mouth of the horse are sufficient for bringing out all of the obedience that the hand should want to elicit. The quality of the rider's hand must be superior to the quality of the bridle and bit. The influence of the bridle must be secondary [to the hand] for the bars of the horse's mouth and the groove of the chin are too tender to sustain abuse, without being altered or crippled by the effects of a bridle that is too harsh and evilly used.

Before explaining the effects of the bridle, we will start by describing all the parts that it is composed of. I would say first that the terms *mors* (bit), *embouchure* (mouthpiece) [both mean mouthpiece] and "bridle" are synonymous depending on their use; technically the bridle is generic and bit is specifically the part that is in the mouth.

The bridle is composed of three main parts which are the bit placed in the mouth of the horse, the shanks that are attached at the ends of the bit and the curb chain that works on the chin.

FIRST ARTICLE

Of the Bit

The bit is a rounded piece of metal that we put in the mouth of the horse that we commonly call the canon or mouthpiece. Both extremities of the mouthpiece where the *branches* (shanks) are attached are called *fonceaux* (end joints) and the part located between the *fonceau* and the middle of the mouthpiece is called *talon* (heel).

In the past we used many kinds of *talons*, which the structure was singular and dangerous for the mouth of the horse; but now we recognized three of them, four at most. They are the *simple canon* [jointed bit], *le canon à trompe ou à canne* (bar bent in the middle), *le canon à liberté de langue* (bit with a port for the freedom of the tongue) and *le pas d'âne* (the ass's step).

The *simple canon* is composed of two parts, because it is jointed in the middle, which gives it more play. It is also the softest of all the bits and the one that offends the mouth of the horse the least.

Le *canon à trompe* (straight bar) is not jointed in the middle and is composed of only one piece which makes it more severe than the *simple canon*.

The *canon à liberté de langue* (the ported cannon) is the one that has an empty space in the center to accommodate the horse's tongue. The degree of freedom of the tongue depends on the shape of the port. There are many types like *gorge de pigeon* [pigeon-throat], *canon montant* [rising cannon] and *pas d'âne* (ass step).

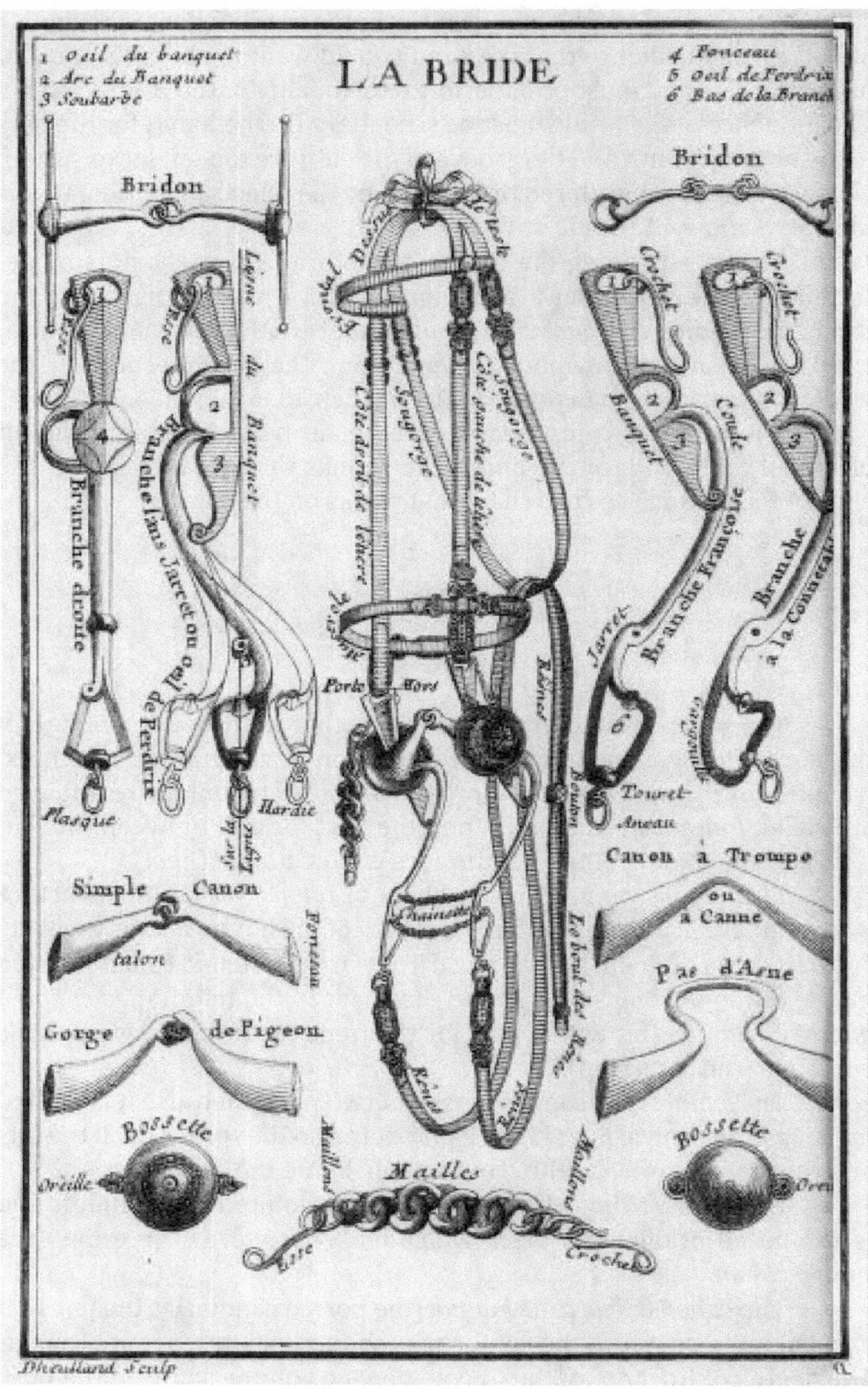

The Bridle

The *canon à gorge de pigeon* (pigeon throat) is the one that the empty, elevated port in the middle of the mouthpiece tapers toward the top. There are pigeon throats with mouthpiece that are jointed or non-jointed. When the port is higher than the *gorge de pigeon*, it is called *canon montant*. The rise of the port is proportionate to the thickness of the tongue.

The *pas d'âne* is a mouthpiece which has a port that is larger and more pronounced then the *gorge du pigeon*. It is not jointed in the middle. This mouthpiece is a remnant of the old severe bits that we must abolish. It is only used in some carriage horses.

There are a few *pas d'âne à liberté gagnée*, (ass step with port) some are jointed and some are not. They are called *Col d'oye* [goose neck]; the port is larger and more crushed than the *pas d'âne*. I would not recommend the use of either one of these bits.

ARTICLE II

Of the Branche (Shank)

The *branche*, which serves to move the mouthpiece, is attached to it by the *fonceaux*, is composed of the *banquet*, the eye of the banquet, the arc of the banquet; of the *soubarbe*; the *coude* (elbow); the *jarret* (calf); the bottom of the branche (shank); the *touret* (fitting where the ring is attached); rings and chains.

The banquet and the top of the shank is also composed of two parts: the eye of the banquet and arc of the banquet.

The eye of the banquet is the hole at the top of the shank through which passes the bottom strap of the cheek piece; it also where the curb chain is attached.

The arc of the banquet is the part that is in the shape of an arc into which is inserted both extremities of the bit. This part is hidden by the *bossette* [boss, or ornamental joint cover], these joint covers are attached by two ears which form the extremities. One must know the top ear is attached to the eye of the banquet and the bottom ear is attached to the part called the *soubarbe*.

The *Coude* (elbow) is the place under the arc of the banquet that is in shape of an "S." The straight *branches* [shanks] also called *branches à pistolets* or *Buades*, do not have an elbow.

The *Jarret* (calf) is at the middle of the *branche* (shank) above the *coude* (elbow).

The bottom of the *branche* (shank) is the empty space you will find below the *Jarret* (calf) and above the *touret* (ring fitting).

The *Touret*, is a nail at the bottom of the shank with a big head twisted over that will hold the ring in which the reins are inserted.

Two small chains are attached to both *branches* (shanks) each by two little *tourets*. For the carriage horses, instead of small chains there is usually a thin metal bar that holds the *branches* (shanks) and the bit together.

Previously, there was no eye at the top of the *branche* (shank) and the curb chain was attached above the mouthpiece, as can be seen in Genette and Moresque mouthpieces.

Currently, there are four types of *branches* (shanks) in use; they are the straight *branche* (shank) also called *à Pistolet* or *Buade*: the French *branche* (shank), the *branche* (shank) without the *Jarret* otherwise called *l'oeil de perdrix* (partridge eye) and the *branche* (shank) of *Connêtable*.

The straight *branche* (shank) or *à Pistolet*, also called *Buade* named after the person who invented it, is the one we use for young horses because there is less constraint and because it usually has longer *branches* (shanks) which renders the mouthpiece softer. The subjection coming from farther does not constrain the horse rudely, while a shorter *branche* (shank) has a more sudden effect.

The French *branche* (shank) is the one that has a *Jarret* in the middle which interrupts the contour.

The branche without the *jarret*, also called *oeil de perdrix* (partridge eye), has an a contour uninterrupted by the *Jarret* and what we call *oeil de perdrix* (partridge eye) is the hole used to set the *touret* that will hold the small chain.

The *branche à la Connêctable* is different from the French *branche* (shank) only by the bottom of the *branche*, because the *gargouille* (which is the part in front of the base of the *branche*) is much longer and curves underneath, which makes the hole of the *touret* set behind. On the other *branches* (shanks) the hole of the *touret* is directly at the bottom of the *branche* (shank). It was named *à la Connêtable* because it was the invention of M. le Connêtable de Montmorenci, the best horseman of his time.

There is again an old *branche* (shank) recently came back fashionable; it's a type of mouthpiece *à la Housarde*, which the *branche* (shank) is very short and has only one small chain. It exists in different shapes, like the others *branches* (shanks), sometime twisted as an S, sometimes straight and sometimes with the hole of the *touret* underneath. This *branche* (shank) might be used by small horses or race horses because it is lighter than the other *branches* (shanks).

We judge the effect of the *branche* (shank) by the line of the *banquet*, which is a lead line that we pull from the top and alongside of the *banquet* all the way to the bottom of the *branche* (shank) which will determine its strength or its weakness. Therefore a *branche* (shank) is harsh, limp or on the line.

The harsh *branche* (shank) is the one that has the hole of the *touret* in front of the line of the *banquet* which means that the bottom of the *branche* is pushed forward. Thus augmenting more or less the effect of the mouthpiece depending if it is more or less harsh.

The *branche* (shank) that we call limp, is the one that has the hole of the *touret* behind the line of the banquet, which is set backward. This will lessen the effect on the mouthpiece proportionally if it is more or less limp.

The *branche* (shank) on the line, is the one that is neither harsh or limp, neither pushed forward nor back, but on the line of the *banquet*.

ARTICLE III

On the Gourmette (CURB CHAIN)

The *Gourmette* (curb chain) is a chain composed of *maille* (links), *maillons* (thinner links), an S and a hook.

The *mailles* that make the chain have to be bigger and thicker in the middle than at the ends.

The *maillons*, which are the thinner links with the thicker links are toward the extremities with two on the side of the hook and one on the side of the S.

The S is the part of the curb chain which is held by a flat soldered link that is attached to the right eye of the *banquet*.

The hook is the part that is held by the right eye of the banquet on the side of the attachment that is used to put on the curb and it enters in one of the two flat soldered that are on that side.

In the past, we used flat curb chain but we found out that the round thick curbs were softer.

ARTICLE IV

The Manner to Direct the Bridle According to the Difference in Mouths.

One must adjust the mouthpiece according to the internal structure of the horse's mouth, the *branches* (shanks) in proportion to his neck, and the curb chain according to the sensibility of his chin.

The mouthpiece must be carried on the bit seat, half a finger above the hook and sometimes one finger according to the way the mouth is split. If he were to carry it too high, it would wrinkle the lip and offend the bone of the bit seat which is more sharp in that part than closer to the hook. One must also be aware the place where the part of the mouthpiece that sits on the bit seat is not in the opening we give to the port. It must apply at half of a finger from the *talon*, which are the extremities of the port, otherwise it will hurt the tongue and the bit seat that is why it is important to choose a mouthpiece of the correct width for the horse's mouth. Furthermore, so that the mouthpiece is sitting at the proper location that the mouthpiece is straight from the fold of the *banquet* about one and a half inch up to the part where the port starts, otherwise the action would be falsified in the mouth. Also the lip of the horse must be so exactly lodged that it prevents from seeing the mouthpiece. The parts composing the mouthpiece must be clean and well-joined in fear of hurting the lip or offending the bit seat.

The size of the mouthpiece must be well-proportioned to the slit [clear space] of the mouth. When one gives too much metal to a mouth of a small opening, it will necessarily wrinkle the lip and, even if the mouth has a larger slit, and the mouthpiece is not big enough, it will be too forward in the mouth ; that is called *boire la bride* (drink the bridle).

One must give to the horse with a good mouth a simple *canon* (jointed without port) with a *branche* (shank) on the line. Even though a good mouth is not as easily offended by mouthpieces, it is always better to give him a soft one, in order to conserve this good quality.

Understand that by good mouth is meant one that has a firm but light support, therefore he does not get upset by the firm motion of a good hand, nor by other movements one must do in order to help the horse.

The more difficult mouths to fit the mouthpiece to, are the mouths that are too tender or lost; weak or too strong; too heavy; too much or not enough slit, the ones that the chin too small, too flat or too elevated, and finally the ones that make a horse brace.

Mouths Too Sensitive

The mouth that is too sensitive is the one that gets easily offended by all kinds of bridles. This sensitivity is recognizable when, at the slightest hand movement, the horse shakes the bridle, jerks his head and wrestles the hand; that is what normally happens to horses who have a bit seat high and sharp. The tongue finding itself lodged in the channel can't support the mouthpiece which is having too much effect on the bit seat, and makes the horse throw his head. The head tossing may also be coming from injuries and ulcers on the bit seat, caused by an ill-adjusted mouthpiece and often by a bad hand. Sometimes also the curb chain may injure the chin, a part that is just as sensitive as the bit seat for certain horses. In these cases, one must wait until the injury is healed and consolidated before thinking of putting a mouthpiece back in the horse's mouth. If the bit seat has been so seriously injured, that a section of the bone has chipped, even though good medicine and nature has refilled the cavity, this section will always remain more sensitive and subject to be offended.

Several horsemen have used the *canon à trompe* (single bar no joint in the middle) as a mouthpiece for horses with a sensitive mouth and who jerk their head, because they say that this mouthpiece not being jointed and all in one piece is supported evenly everywhere and has, as a consequence, a soothing effect. As far as I am concerned, I agree with the ones who say that it would be more appropriate to use the simple canon (jointed mouthpiece) that does not have too much play. Therefore it would have the strength of the *canon à trompe* but the gentleness of the *simple canon* (jointed). In order to make it even gentler, it should be thicker close to the *fonceaux* (ends of the mouthpiece) as much as the natural opening of the mouth allows it and must have little lift, meaning that the joint does not rise too high and tickle the roof of the mouth.

The eye of the *banquet* (top part of the shank) should be a little lower, slightly reversed and bend backward to diminish the effect of the curb chain. Note that the higher the eye is, the more action you have on the curb chain.

Regarding the kind of *branche* (shank) that suits these kind of horses, we shall choose one with an easy curve, on the line and a little longer. One should note, as we stated previously, that a longer *branche* (shank) restrains less than a shorter one because it reaches more easily the chest therefore creates a release at the bit seat and diminishes the support of the mouthpiece.

Weak Mouths

The weak mouth is one that does not accept the support of any mouthpieces, that has great difficulty, no matter how soft the bit is, even without any provocation from the hand. Horses who have this problem should be fitted with the same type of mouthpiece as the ones with sensitive mouths which is a *simple canon* (jointed mouthpiece), the *branche* (shank) on the line and a bit longer and mostly with a lower eye (at the top of the shank).

Those who believe, as we have just said, that correcting the sensitive or weak mouths with a *canon à trompe* (unjointed straight bar) are wrong; since this mouthpiece is naturally severe and consequently wakes up the bars, it is only adequate for mouths that have lost their natural sensitivity and for carriage horses, who need stronger mouthpieces than mounted horses.

Strong Mouths

We understand by strong mouth the horse who pulls on your hands. This harshness normally comes from either the thickness of the tongue, the lips and the gums which cover the bit seat and interfere with the action of the mouthpiece, or that the bit seat is too round or too low. Sometimes a horse will pull on the hands because of too much impetuosity and apprehension or shortness of breath. In these latter cases, we must appease him with good lessons and give him a bridle suited to the structure of his mouth.

But if he pulls the hand because of a large tongue, thick lips or rounded bit seat, we must give him a mouth a *canon à gorge de pigeon*, the one with a port. Then the tongue being freed, can lodged itself in the space in the middle of the mouthpiece where the port is and the mouthpiece will be able to act on the bit seat. Mouthpieces with ports have this advantage, it keeps the tongue from going over the top of the bit.

In order to make these mouths even more responsive, the mouthpiece must not be too big, instead, there should be less metal toward the ends of the mouthpiece and sized sensibly to the size of the slit of the mouth.

Regarding the *branche* (shank), it should be a little shorter and stronger but not too much. Wanting to over-constrain a horse who carries his head high, will, instead of bringing him into the *ramener*, cause him to pull even more.

Heavy Mouths

A horse is normally heavy on the hand when the bit seat is thick, fleshy and low; too big of a tongue, a faulty and heavy neck, jaws too square and tight. Often the horse has a heavy head by weakness, either of the feet, the loin or the hips which makes these kind of horses apprehensive of their strength therefore leaning on the mouthpiece and using it as a fifth leg. In this case the bridle is not the solution. Often there are horses leaning in the hand by bad habit, by ignorance and by laziness; then one must recourse to the art.

If the horse is heavy in the hand because of fat tongue and lips or rounded, low bit seat, you must give him the same mouthpiece as the one who pulls which is a thinner *canon à george de pigeon* with a port that is proportioned to the size of his tongue. He also needs a branche (shank) without the Jarret, a little harsher and the eye a little higher than the ones who pull in your hand to augment the strength on the curb chain which should not be so big as the regular ones because these kind of horses have normally a thicker chin.

Mouths with Too Little or Too Long Slits

We have mentioned above that too much metal in a small slit mouth will cause wrinkles and that a mouthpiece to skinny would go too much forward in a long-slitted mouth. Keeping in mind these principles, it is easy to fix these faults with the simple aspect of the mouth structure. One must pay attention with the strong mouths to proportion the eye (of the shank) to the slit so that it would be lower for the long slit mouth and higher for the short ones and that is for this very distinct reason which is if the eye was too high and the mouth too big, the curb chain would get over while asking the horse to come back. If the slit of the mouth was too small and the eye too low, the curb chain would hang.

Horses Which Arm [Brace]

The most difficult mouths to bit are the ones of horses that arm, because in a bridle there is no action that directly pushes the nose of the horse forward. Its only action is to hold and shorten the action of the horse.

Horses brace in two ways: the ones with a long slender and overly-supple neck, will round their neck, lower their forehead and touch the shank against the chest therefore rendering the mouthpiece ineffective.

The others are the ones with an inverted neck, tense throat latch and full of large muscles that prevent the jaw from taking its normal position, even more if the latter part is too tight. On these horses the shanks lean on the throat, preventing the effects of the mouthpiece and curb chain.

Whichever way a horse braces, one must give him a very gentle mouthpiece, with lower eyes, for a harsh mouthpiece would create more bracing since he falls in this flaw to avoid the subjection of the mouthpiece.

The *branches à la Housarde*, as previously discussed, fitted with a mouthpiece suited to the inside shape of the mouth work fairly well in correcting horses who brace by leaning the shank against the throat. The bridoon (double jointed snaffle) is good to defeat the ones who *s'encapuchonnent* [over-flex].

Regarding the curb chain, it should be big for the horses with a small, raised or sensitive chin so as not to damage that part, and correspondingly not as big for a fleshy, hairy chin in order to wake up this area.

In all curb chains the S and the hook must be well-made, they should be curved to conform and follow the roundness of the lip and should descend all the way to the *coude* (elbow) of the shank, otherwise they will pinch the lip and offend this area.

Another absolutely necessary attention is to know how to set the curb chain on the flat side so it does not hurt the chin. Of all three sides of the curb chain, they are two with the links which form the chain, are split and the third one are not. If it is the side that the links are not split are toward the outside then the curb chain is on the flat side.

When the horse's chin is too sensitive, we add felt sheath around the curb chain like a piece from an old hat or leather the length of two thumbs [two inches or more]. It must be the whole length of the curb chain at the extremities so we can pass the chain through it so that it lays between the chin and the curb chain. This will relieve the chin groove and reduces the harshness of the curb chain.

It is not sufficient just to know all of the types of mouthpieces and bits for the wide variety of horses and the many different types of equine mouths. No matter how good the complete bridle is fitted, without a good hand on the part of the rider, and without enough prudence in the rider, that bridle will be rendered useless.

It is primarily by the art which reaffirms good lessons wisely practiced and secondarily by a bridle that does not offend any part of the horse's mouth, that one arrives at training a horse.

www.ingramcontent.com/pod-product-compliance
Lightning Source LLC
Chambersburg PA
CBHW060513300426
44112CB00017B/2651